Resources for Teaching Shakespeare 11–16

Also available from Continuum

Resources for Teaching English 11–14, Helena Ceranic
Resources for Teaching English 14–16, David A. Hill
Resources for Teaching Creative Writing, Johnnie Young

Resources for Teaching Shakespeare 11–16

Fred Sedgwick

continuum

A companion website to accompany this book is available online at:
http://education.sedgwick.continuumbooks.com
Please visit the link and register with us to receive your password and to access these downloadable resources.
If you experience any problems accessing the resources, please contact Continuum at:
info@continuumbooks.com

Continuum International Publishing Group

The Tower Building   80 Maiden Lane, Suite 704
11 York Road   New York, NY 10038
London
SE1 7NX

www.continuumbooks.com

British Library Cataloguing-in-Publication Data
A catalogue record for this book is available from the British Library.

ISBN: 978-0-8264-3859-1 (paperback)

Library of Congress Cataloging-in-Publication Data
Sedgwick, Fred.
Resources for teaching shakespeare 11–16 / Fred Sedgwick.
     p. cm.
   ISBN 978-0-8264-3859-1 – ISBN 978-1-4411-8077-3 – ISBN 978-1-4411-4188-0 1. Drama in education. 2. Drama–Study and teaching (Primary) 3. Drama–Study and teaching (Secondary) I. Title.

PN3171.S33 2011
822.3'3–dc22   2011000392

Typeset by Pindar NZ, Auckland, New Zealand
Printed and bound in India

Contents

With thanks to Colin
To the memory of Henry Thornton Grammar School

Introduction

Any civilised man growing up in England needs to know his Shakespeare.

Ridiculous now – but, no more than a hundred and fifty years ago – that statement would have been unarguable. Alongside the Bible and the myths of Ancient Greece and Rome, Shakespeare was part of every educated man's intellectual luggage.

There were dissenting views, of course. George III said (so Fanny Burney records in her diary) 'Was there ever such stuff as great as part of Shakespeare? Only one must not say so!' And he was expressing with regal privilege what was thought by most of his court: one can't imagine his Prince Regent, later George IV, being anything but bored by the plays and the poems. And later, Charles Darwin found Shakespeare 'nauseous'. And later still: '*King Lear*? Never read it, never seen it': a history lecturer said this to me with a bland smile over lunch at college forty years ago.

Hamlet tells his friend Horatio that Elsinore's carousing custom would be 'More honour'd in the breach than the observance'. One suspects that much honouring of Shakespeare was – is – done so. The myth of Shakespeare – the supreme Englishman, up there with the Duke of Wellington and Lord Nelson – was built more on an iconic status than his work. There's that domed forehead, that soft beard and moustache, those steady eyes.

Today, both that phrase 'civilised man' and that word 'England', with their different modes of exclusion, would be laughed at in an educational context, as in most others. And that change is only one among many. A 'civilised' man a couple of centuries ago would have been, with notable and rare exceptions, an aristocrat; later, he might have been aspiring middle class. But in a society like our own, most of us who have any interest in the subject recognise that Shakespeare is for everyone. Not just for men, not just for the aristocracy, not just for the powerful middle classes finding their way through the public schools, or manipulating their way through the state sector; not just for the grammar school children of the years after World War II (such as myself), not just the well-behaved in modern comprehensives; not just for the English, or even those with English as their first language. Everyone is owed, at the very least, a taste of the works of Shakespeare because of (if for no other reason) the delight they can give.

For those of us who feel this delight, how did it begin? My brother Colin, another child of the expansion of state grammar schools in the wake of the Butler Education Act of 1944, writes:

> It undoubtedly started for me when I was given a job in my first year at grammar school in a production of *Henry IV Part 1*. It meant me heading off to round up the actors for the next scene(s). As a result there were certain chunks of the play that I heard over and over again, so much so that they are lodged for ever in my memory ('I can call spirits from the vasty deep . . .'). Another spine-tingling line was Hal, upbraided by his father for his dissolute lifestyle, kneeling and declaring 'I shall hereafter, my thrice-noble lord, be more myself'. The power of words!

The school that my brother and I attended organised a trip to see the same play. I remember seeing Judi Dench at the Old Vic sometime in the 1960s as Lady Percy, and hearing the lines, spoken by the prince (John Stride, I think – I had not begun my collection of Shakespeare theatre programmes) to Falstaff:

> What a devil hast thou to do with the time of day? Unless hours were cups of sack, and minutes capons, and clocks the tongues of bawds, and dials the signs of leaping-houses, and the blessed sun himself a fair hot wench in flame-coloured taffeta . . .

And even though I didn't have a clue what a leaping-house was, or how taffeta looked or felt, and although my idea of a bawd was pretty hazy, I was drawn in. I type the passage out now with line breaks at each comma and after 'himself':

> What a devil hast thou to do with the time of day?
> Unless hours were cups of sack,
> and minutes capons,
> and clocks the tongues of bawds,
> and dials the signs of leaping-houses,
> and the blessed sun himself
> a fair hot wench in flame-coloured taffeta . . .

Looking at the lines, I see such vigour in the rhythm of the speech: a rhythm like a modern poem's: the way the first four short clauses of the second sentence, from 'Unless' to 'houses', prepare the reader or listener in steps for the lovely climax about 'the blessed sun'; how the sudden drop into a description of a prostitute (a disturbingly glamorous sounding one) has a comic bathos; how authentic the rhythms of this speech are – the speech of a powerful man patronising a companion.

Of course, I saw (or rather heard) none of this when I was at school. Now, examining lines like this does not take away the 'magic' (as people often say it does). It sharpens it. That is why, in this book, I have set out to help students to see the way Shakespeare's language is working.

Both these stories – my brother's and mine – have two things in common. First, our experiences were generated by teachers. Someone had given up his (it was an all-boys school) time and talent to produce the school play, and did it, probably, every year; and someone – quite likely the same person – had taken a party of schoolboys to the theatre (the Old Vic). Second, the teachers were working outside classrooms – in a real theatre, and in a school hall doing a good imitation of one. All too often, teachers and students are locked (or, in the case of teachers, lock themselves) in the relatively arid atmosphere of the classroom, when a different environment – a theatre or, in the case of *A Midsummer Night's Dream* or *As You Like It*, the open air might be more appropriate (though I would not recommend a blasted heath for the study of *Macbeth*, or working in a 'pitiless storm' to study *King Lear*).

As teachers today, many of us underrate our influence on students. First, there is so much competition: media, for example, developed to a sophistication that would have bamboozled us in our youth – even those of us in the profession only a few years. We can't compete with modern communication; with entertainment; with the way the society of the young operates. Facebook and Twitter take up so much space in their lives that anything Miss or Sir says comes (we assume) low down on their list of priorities.

Second, my travels around schools tell me something even more powerful is knocking at the self-confidence of teachers: constant changes imposed from above, reams and reams of paper to be read, with lines of blank spaces to be filled in. The clerical work seems to most of the profession to be at best irrelevant and at worst downright wicked. This profession is hampered, hidebound, harassed every day. Those of us who have given lifetimes to this profession know that there is little point is railing against this state of affairs; that the only way forward is to understand that the teacher and the student are the only people who ultimately matter, and to practise our calling in the light of that understanding. Teacher, student: we are central to what education is . . . and the best teachers are students, and all the best students are teachers. And Shakespeare's words, and the study of them, re-assert our humanity.

No one, as the critic Harold Bloom (1999) has written, 'made so many separate selves' as Shakespeare. This is an exaggeration – what about Dickens, what about Trollope? And what about literature in other languages? But Bloom makes a telling point. Even in the three plays on which this book focuses we find a neurotic careerist with a poetic heart, a wife driven by her own ambition to lunacy and a drunken cynic at the gates of Hell; we find a bumbling mangler of words full of good humour, decency and self-knowledge, four self-deceiving lovers and two honest ones; we find an immature male and a wiser female in her early teens tossed between tribal rivalries, a maddened poet who must die young, a priest with all the wisdom of a fool, and that timeless pair, controlling parents. The plays of Shakespeare can teach us, if we listen and read and look, much of what it is to be a human being.

My brother's story and mine have something else in common besides an inspired teacher: they are each about plays. Shakespeare is a playwright. He is not a purveyor of texts to be pored over and annotated, a Tudor equivalent of Sudoku. It is more than possible to treat his words in this second way, of course, and most adults that I speak to provide sad evidence of this. Their stories about studying Shakespeare at school explain their negativity towards the plays once they are adults. They remember reading the plays round the class without any sense of drama and fun, for example; and at a higher level, treating the plays as texts to be examined, explained, compared, rather than scripts to be enjoyed, to be produced.

Something else that my anecdotes share is a relish of the *language* of Shakespeare. Many good writers, from Charles Lamb onwards (*Tales from Shakespeare*, 1807, written with his sister Mary) have re-told the tales. But the liveliest opening sentence of a story based on *Macbeth*, written in however up-to-date a style, however dark and brisk, however commanding, however violent, will, firstly, have nothing of Shakespeare in it. Here is Shakespeare's language:

> What bloody man is that? He can report,
> As seemeth by his plight, of the revolt
> The newest state.

Macbeth Act 1 Scene 2

I am assuming here that Shakespeare wasn't singly responsible for the actual first lines, though they are hard to beat too:

> FIRST WITCH: When shall we three meet again?
> In thunder, lighting, or in rain?

Teaching Shakespeare's stories is not teaching Shakespeare. He wrote almost none of them: *Macbeth*, for example, is taken largely from Ralph Holinshed's account of the reigns of Duncan and Macbeth (Holinshed is also largely responsible for the mythically evil, hunchbacked *Richard III*, and for the heroic *Henry V*; and for most of the material in the English history plays). *Romeo and Juliet* is based on various Italian stories. *A Midsummer Night's Dream* is an exception among these plays, and very rare in the whole canon, in that it is almost all Shakespeare's own invention; but even here, he draws on Chaucer (*The Knight's Tale*).

Today, any writer – novelist or playwright – is assumed, usually rightly, to be responsible for everything – characterisation, dialogue, narrative style – and plot; otherwise, we have a plagiarist on our hands. It requires a significant mental leap for students to understand that taking an old story and making it new, making it theirs, was what playwrights did (no novelists around then). And that it was (and is, or can be) as creative an act as dreaming up stories. More so, in fact.

In *Shakespeare and the Young Writer* (1999), a concern for teaching students the language of the plays rather than the plots led me to concentrate too much on the poet. I gave insufficient weight to the idea of the playwright, and in this book, I present ideas that enable students to see both Shakespeare the poet – the man whose plays are full of, for example, lyric poetry, arguably some of the greatest that has ever been written in the language –

> Tomorrow, and tomorrow, and tomorrow
> Creeps in this petty pace from day to day
> To the last syllable of recorded time;
> And all our yesterdays have lighted fools
> The way to dusty death. Out, out, brief candle,
> Life's but a walking shadow, a poor player
> That struts and frets his hour upon the stage

And then is heard no more. It is a tale
Told by an idiot, full of sound and fury
Signifying nothing.

– and Shakespeare the craftsman, the man who (discussing and arguing about his scripts with actors and other collaborators) turned old stories into plays, knowing the next one must be ready by next Thursday; but who, in doing so, wrote plays, as it appeared to Ben Jonson, and as it appears to us, 'not for an age, but for all time'.

Using this book

This book presents forty-one pairs of sheets: sixteen pairs for *Macbeth*, twelve for *A Midsummer Night's Dream* and thirteen for *Romeo and Juliet*. The left-hand side of each pair is a teacher's sheet, and the right-hand side is a task sheet for students. A relevant passage from the play is given online, and at the back of this book, as a focus point for the lesson. But it must be said: I have assumed that, first, the students have copies of the play to hand and, second, that they know the stories (sometimes the task sheets give hints about the endings).

The teacher's sheet is made up like this: an introduction; a statement of intended aims; a starter; a main phase of about 35–45 minutes; and a plenary. The whole lesson should take about an hour, but all times are flexible. They have to be, because of the nature of school life (I could have written, 'because of the nature of life'). Sometimes there will be more time available, and the starter can expand; and sometimes less, and the main phases can be shortened, or the plenary abandoned. As for 'aims': most of us know that in many of our best lessons students learn something that we didn't intend them to learn; or they learn something that we had not thought through sufficiently to be framed in that reductive notion 'aims'. And often a student's comment leads discussion into a path that we hadn't thought of. So the aims section is always provisional. (Like aims in life.)

The task sheets are made up of exercises designed to reinforce learning. The tasks are arranged in approximate ascending order of difficulty, though sometimes, when they are about the same character – Friar Lawrence, say – I have grouped them together without reference to their difficulty. I have resisted the use of the term 'differentiation' because I find it impossible to use in my writing without making unwarrantable judgements about students whom I don't know. Expectations are everything. As a travelling writer I can treat students as enthusiasts for Shakespeare until they prove that they are not. I can only council a perfection, and hope that teachers, familiar as they will be with their students' reputations, will expect the best.

Gender roles

In Shakespeare's time, Lady Macbeth, Juliet and her Nurse, and Titania, Hyppolita and the female lovers – Helena and Hermia – were acted, almost certainly, by adolescent boys. Juliet wasn't played by a woman until 1662, nearly half a century after Shakespeare's death. We can catch a glimpse of an all-male cast in the rehearsals for the play within *A Midsummer Night's Dream* (1.2), where Flute protests: 'Nay, faith, let me not play a woman: I have a beard coming'. In *Twelfth Night* we have the exotic sight (give it some thought) of a male actor playing a female pretending to be a male (Viola/Cesare), and the same happens in *Cymbeline* (male actor/Imogen/Fidele). When Shakespeare wrote, in Sonnet 20, about, or rather to, 'thou, the master-mistress of my passion', he was drawing on some part of his psychology certainly, but he was also drawing, less mysteriously, on his experience in the theatre.

Almost every production since Restoration times has played fast and loose with Shakespearean convention by using female actors to play women and male actors to play men. This fact alone, even if we need no other, is licence for us today not to be hidebound by that more recent convention: they broke the rules, why shouldn't we? In the classroom (and in any bigger space that might be available for playing with Shakespeare's scripts) male students should sometimes speak female roles and vice versa. This practice often exposes dimensions that are otherwise closed to us. Listen to a male Lady Macbeth, for example, when she initiates the central action of the play (1.5) as she speaks the lines '. . . unsex me here / And fill me from the crown to the toe topfull / Of direst cruelty . . .'

By treating the scripts in this way, we open up valuable discussion. In 1998, Rex Gibson could write:

> School . . . students have no difficulty in sharing feminism's recognition that Shakespeare's female characters merit equal attention with male characters . . .

And while this may be true, since 1998 relations between the sexes (especially as experienced by young people) have become more defined within traditional roles. There's been a change of gear. Society has engaged reverse. In almost all advertising aimed at the young, in all magazines and in any talent show on weekend television, young women are displayed as sex objects. And not just the young. The host of a popular TV programme (Simon Cowell) recently asked a middle-aged, female contestant (Susan Boyle) 'What do you want to be, my dear?' *My* dear? My *dear*?

Lady Macbeth and Hyppolita, among other women, offer chances to explore and criticise accepted norms about sexual policies, not as they are theorised about, but as they are lived; and experimenting in the classroom or the rehearsal room with different ways of playing them provokes thought and discussion about gender roles today. And varying who plays their roles (not always males as in Shakespeare's time, not almost always females as in ours) enhances this thought, this discussion.

Young people can make Shakespeare's words theirs. They do this by playing with them and studying them – two activities not as different from each other as might be supposed – and by that play and that study, they become more informed about what it meant to be human in Shakespeare's time, and what it means to be human in their own time. They will be better fitted to address many issues that are central to being a civilised human being.

Key to icon

There is one icon, which appears throughout the text.

Resources available online.

Section 1   *Macbeth*

Lost and won

Act 1 Scene 1, lines 1–11: available online and at the end of this book.

Introduction

Most students will be familiar with the witches, so one potential problem is a stereotype: hags with rags, brooms, pointed hats, cats, cackles. Ask the students to forget Halloween, and to banish such images from their minds.

Aims

The students will understand how the weird sisters' speeches in 1.1 introduce a central theme of the play. They will be ready to examine later speeches by the witches (1.3; 3.5; 4.1). They will have experience of performing part of a Shakespearean script, and they will begin to understand how certain words are keywords to a line, a speech, a scene, an act, a play.

Starter (10 minutes)

Suggest that the class abandons the use of the word 'witch' and that they substitute the term 'weird sister'. Point out that this is the name that the 'witches' use for themselves, and ask them, for homework, to find this term (1.3, line 30).

Ask the students to act 1.1 as a radio play with friends. They should avoid cackling: what other voices might be appropriate? They should do it again, with different voices and different emphases.

Main phase (45 minutes)

Point out that Shakespeare plays with opposites and contradictions in these lines: 'lost, and won'; 'fair is foul, and foul is fair'. (See later, Lesson 7: Here's a knocking indeed, and Lesson 30: *Romeo and Juliet* and Oxymorons, p. 95). Gather from the students other contradictions from modern speech: 'friendly fire' as used by the US military. Introduce the word 'oxymoron'. Ask the students to make a list of their own oxymorons.

Point out that 'lost, and won' has an obvious meaning: someone will lose the battle, and someone else will win it. But there is another possible meaning: could the same person both win and lose?

Contradictions: the weird sisters introduce one central theme of the play. Ask the students to scour the script to find other contradictions, and to discover who speaks them. Some references are:

> 'Lost and won'. 1.2.66 Duncan
>
> 'Fair is foul'. 1.3.36 Macbeth
>
> 'Lesser' and 'greater' 1.3.63 First Witch
>
> 'Not so happy, yet much happier' Second Witch in the next line.
>
> 'joys' and 'sorrows' 1.4.3–35 Duncan
>
> 'harm / Is laudable . . . good . . . dangerous folly' 4.2.73–74 Lady Macduff

Suggest your possible 'keyword' (see task sheet) for the second speech: 'Hurly-burly'? 'Battle'? 'Lost'?

Plenary (5 minutes)

Revise and discuss issues already raised: contradictions, keywords.

Lost and won

Act 1 Scene 1, lines 1–11

1 Draw a costume for a weird sister that would surprise an audience when the curtain goes up, and yet seem right.

2 Commit to memory any of the following of the weird sisters' speeches: 1.3.1–12; 1.3.13–24; 1.3.25–35.

3 Arrange yourselves in three roughly equal groups. One group represents FIRST WITCH. The others represent SECOND and THIRD WITCHES.

* Learn your lines. Individually, decide what you think is the keyword for your witch, or weird sister: the one most full of meaning. There is no single right answer: yours is the right one as long as you can justify your choice. Discuss your choices.

* Now, as a class – one third for each weird sister – speak the lines, as if for a radio play. No actions are needed.

4 Break into smaller groups of three, with one student from each third in each threesome. Convert the radio play into a stage play. Before you do, here are some questions:

* How would you have the weird sisters enter? Together? From different directions?

* What is their relationship to each other? Are they true friends? Do they trust, or distrust, each other?

* How can body language suggest the nature of their relationships?

* Suggest possibly answers these to these questions, and design your play appropriately.

5 Lost and won

* 'Lost and won'. Find this pairing somewhere else in Act 1 Scene 2.

* 'Fair is foul'. And find this one, somewhere in Act 1.

* Look out for other contradictions throughout the play. Find as many as you can. Make notes of these, because they are central to understanding *Macbeth*.

* If you don't know already, find out the meaning of 'oxymoron'. Make up a few oxymorons of your own.

6 Be different!

* Most of us, when we think of witches, think immediately of women, older than anyone's grandmother, with hooked, pointed noises, straggly hair and tall black hats.

* Make a list of other ways in which we might see the weird sisters. In one production, the weird sisters weren't seen at all: they spoke in hoarse whispers throughout from off-stage.

* In past productions, the weird sisters have been seen as:
  — elegantly dressed ladies laughing among themselves
  — masked dancers
  — visible from only their necks down.

* Do they have to be female? In Shakespeare's time they were played by males. Indeed someone in the play – find out who – has noticed that they have beards.

* The word 'witch' is only used once throughout the play. It's in Act 1 – find it. Who says it? Macbeth calls them 'weird sisters'.

* When you make your drawings, bear these suggestions in mind.

Killing machine

Act 1 Scene 2, especially lines 7–23: available online and at the end of this book.

Introduction

'Witches' are familiar: that was both an advantage and a disadvantage in 1.1. This scene presents challenges, but it's helpful that no stereotypes are involved. It is important that the students discover the Captain's speech in all its (to coin an oxymoron) 'nasty glamour'.

Images from modern warfare might well illustrate a display about the character Macbeth, alongside an enlarged photocopy of this speech and other quotations from this scene; later, students' responses to the homework tasks would make the display even stronger: their lists of violent scenes from the media, and their similes based on the captain's words: 'As two spent swimmers that do cling together . . .'

Aims

The students will begin to appreciate both the vigour of Shakespeare's writing, and the subtlety of his similes; they will begin to appreciate (through the muscularity of the language) something of Macbeth's abilities as a soldier – and also something vital in his character.

They will be challenged about any views they may have of Shakespeare merely as a purveyor of 'hey nonny no and bloody poetry' (as a student once characterised Shakespeare to me). They will learn how Shakespeare often uses punctuation and line breaks as directions to an actor on how to speak the lines.

Starter (10 minutes)

Begin with line 22, and say it, miming the action, with as much venom as you can muster: 'Till he unseamed him from the nave to the chaps'. Ask: where do we usually use the word 'seam'? It's a term from needlework. After explaining 'chaps' ('jaws') ask the students to visualise what Macbeth does to Macdonald: he rips the body open as a teddy bear's body might be opened by a disturbed child, from the belly to the jaws. Ask the students to examine the rest of the script: 'Upwards . . .'

Main phase (40 minutes)

Ask the students, in groups, to read lines 1–44, underlining or noting down every word that is in any way violent. Ask them to shout the words at each other, taking it in turns in a circle. Suggest that they begin with 'bloody', 'revolt', 'broil', 'choke', 'merciless', 'villainies' . . . There are at least twenty more.

Now, ask each group to prepare a presentation of the lines on their task sheet to the rest of the class that suggest the exhaustion of the speaker.

Now ask them to write the private thoughts of the captain as he rests (at last!) after delivering his news.

Plenary (10 minutes)

Ask the students to brainstorm as many adjectives as they can to describe Macbeth's character as seen in the word picture painted by the Captain, and to keep these adjectives to hand when they come to the next scene.

Glossary

Kerns and galloglasses are, respectively, lightly and heavily armed soldiers. Because the kerns carried little equipment, they found it easier to run away (line 20).

Killing machine

Act 1 Scene 2, especially lines 7–23

1. Learn lines 7–23 by heart, or any group of lines.

2. Make a list of violent scenes from films or television dramas that are comparable to the picture drawn in line 22. Collect images from modern warfare, and find lines in *Macbeth* that could accompany them.

3. 'As two spent swimmers that do cling together / And choke their art': this simile provides a vivid picture of exhausted enemies. Make a drawing to illustrate it, or make other similes that describe the same scenario.

4. In groups, read lines 1–44, noting down every violent word. You might begin with 'bloody', 'revolt', 'broil', 'choke', 'merciless', 'swarm'. Include words that have become swearwords, or insulting words, in our time.

5. In groups, prepare a way of presenting lines 7–44 (the Captain's speech) to everyone else. You should do this first as a radio play.
   - How might you suggest the exhaustion of the speaker? Shakespeare does much of the work for you. Stop and breathe at every punctuation mark, every line ending. It has often been said that Shakespeare provides many of his stage directions in the script. For example,

     Doubtful it stood, [*he gasps for breath*]
     As two spent swimmers . . .

   And the full stop in the third line after '. . . choke their art' might denote a longer and more desperate pause.

6. Once you have performed the lines as a radio play, you might imagine presenting them on stage. Decisions have to be made: how do the other characters react to the Captain – both to the man himself and his plight, and to his story? Differentiate between the King's reactions; those of his two sons, Malcolm and Donaldblain; those of the thane Lennox; and those of the attendants.
   - It would be a boring scene to look at if everyone reacted in the same way, or if everyone just stood there watching the captain speak. Make presentations of this speech.

7. See it from the Captain's point of view: he is exhausted, wounded, in great pain and, for all he knows, on the point of death for most of this scene.
   - Write down his private thoughts as he lies, wounds bandaged, in the field hospital, or what he might say to his family about this scene when recovering. They will make a contrast with what he said to the King!

8. 'Another Golgotha': Look up St. Matthew (27.33). What does this add to the Captain's remark?

9. We haven't seen Macbeth yet, but we have heard a lot about him. Summarise in a page your impressions of him.

10. A critic once described Macbeth as a 'killing machine'. This is an Anglo-Saxon usage called a kenning: a name we might apply to something. A sword, for example, is a 'widow-maker', a telephone a 'far-speaker'.
    - Make a list of kennings to describe Macbeth or the weird sisters.

The milk of human kindness

Act 1 Scene 5, selected lines from 'They met me' to 'murd'ring ministers': available online and at the end of this book.

Introduction

In 1.2, students saw a picture of Macbeth the soldier: a killing machine, capable of unseaming a man's body upwards. Now they see different pictures of him, both in his letter to his wife, and in her soliloquy. Here is a man full of 'the milk of human kindness'.

Aims

The students will see that Shakespeare is immensely subtle in his construction of character: the 'killing machine' can be nervous and introspective (1.3) and even, at least if his wife's comments are anything to go by, full of kindness.

They will form an impression in their minds of the relationship between Macbeth and Lady Macbeth as it appears in this scene. They should be alerted to watch where, later in the play, the relationship changes.

Starter (10 minutes)

Revise what the students already know about Macbeth from the Captain's speech in 1.2, and ask them to look briefly at Macbeth's lines in 1.3, especially line 36. Ask the students to pick out and underline all the phrases in this scene that suggest a gentler Macbeth than the one we have seen, or heard of in hearsay, in battle.

Suggest the following: 'my dearest partner'; 'too full o'the milk of human kindness'. Ask the students: what aspect of Macbeth's character is emerging here?

Main phase (40 minutes)

Ask the students to read, individually, the lines on the task sheet, and to write down words and phrases that describe their first impressions of Lady Macbeth. Ask them to share their words in groups. Then ask them, individually, to write a short pen portrait of the queen.

Point out that the speech in lines 39–52 ('Come, you spirits' to 'Hold, hold!') is a prayer. Ask the students to imagine: to what kind of being is that prayer addressed? Ask them, in groups, to say the prayer in a way that would curdle the blood.

Plenary (10 minutes)

It is best if, in this first hotseating, you take the part of Lady Macbeth.

One person is Lady Macbeth, and sits at the front of the class. The others have to ask the character questions about her motivation, her feelings for Macbeth; ask what she will feel if she carries out her plan. It is important the character in the hot seat answers honestly. It is also important that, if the students take the role, that male students have a chance to take Lady Macbeth's part.

Ask the students to think about the spirits to whom Lady Macbeth addresses her 'prayer', and to write notes to describe what those spirits might be like. They might begin with Lady Macbeth's own description of them: 'murd'ring ministers'.

Ask them to be the director, and to write notes for the actor playing Lady Macbeth: how, for example, does she enter to make the clearest impression of what she is like? How does she bear herself?

Note about the language: 'perfectest' is wrong, in modern terms; 'the milk of human kindness' is just one of the phrases Shakespeare invents that have come down to us. Point these out.

The milk of human kindness

Act 1 Scene 5, selected lines from 'They met me' to 'murd'ring ministers'

1 Line 36 of 1.3 is a central one in this play for understanding Macbeth, the plot and what happens to Lady Macbeth. Learn it by heart.

2 Look at 1.5 lines 1–28. Where is the killing machine now? Pick out all the phrases in this scene that show a different side of Macbeth.

3 Read Lady Macbeth's speech that begins 'The raven . . .' silently. Read it again, aloud. Emphasise all the words that suggest horror, beginning, perhaps, with 'unsex'. Or maybe with 'raven'; it's worth knowing that the raven has often been associated with death. One actor retched as she said 'Unsex me here' as though she had frightened herself with her own words. Work out ways of acting the lines in a radio play from 'Come you spirits', to 'Hold, hold!'

4 That speech is, in fact, a prayer. Imagine to whom it is prayed: what kind of supernatural creature is likely to grant sexlessness (to take just one example) to a woman who asks for it? Make notes about this creature then make a drawing of it.

5 Look at both the passages online or on the board. The phrases 'wrongly win', 'unsex', 'milk for gall', 'murd'ring ministers' describe things the wrong way round: most people would be horrified at the thought of an unsexed woman, or one who wanted her mother's milk to be like 'a secretion of the liver, bile . . . intensely bitter' (that's a dictionary definition of 'gall'). Make a list of all the words in the play so far that worked like this, beginning with 'lost and won' in 1.1. Go as far into the play doing this as you have time for.

6 Earlier on, you were asked to think about the witches in fresh ways. Here is another vision of them: 'they made themselves air, into which they vanished'. Write a poem in which each stanza describes a different version of the witches. Use images from the internet, and from any other source you can find: possibly illustrations in your edition of the play; but mainly words spoken about them by other characters.

7 Macbeth has written 'perfectest' in his letter. It is, of course, wrong: what should it be? How has Shakespeare made such a mistake – or has he?

© Fred Sedgwick, 2011. *Resources for Teaching Shakespeare: 11–16.*

4 A pleasant seat

Act 1 Scene 6, lines 1–14: available online and at the end of this book.

Introduction

Anyone starting to study *Macbeth* with this scene would only see 'a pleasant seat', kindness, loyalty, greetings between a king and his loyal hostess.

But because the students have studied 1.5, they know that, although Lady Macbeth may look like 'the innocent flower', she is in fact 'the serpent under it'.

Aims

The students should begin to understand dramatic irony, and to see another aspect of Lady Macbeth's character – her ability to 'act innocent': her hypocrisy.

Starter (15 minutes)

Banquo talks about the 'martlet' (house martin) who has chosen its 'pendent' (hanging) place to raise its young. It may be necessary to explain what Banquo is saying, and its relevance: even the birds of the air appreciate the Macbeths' hospitality. But it is also worth explaining that a 'martlet' (martin) was a word used for a dupe, a mug, and that, to put it crudely, is what Duncan is here.

Ask the students to read lines 1–14, noting down, or underlining, every word or phrase that signifies anything about friendship, kindness, welcome; they might begin with 'pleasant' and 'nimbly'.

Explain dramatic irony: when 'the development of the plot allows the audience to possess more information about what is happening than some of the characters have' (from *A Dictionary of Literary Terms* by Martin Gray).

Main phase (40 minutes)

Ask the students: How does Lady Macbeth speak these lines? With seeming sincerity? Is she gushing, over-the-top? Or with a manner which betrays (to us if not to the king) her nervousness about what is about to happen? Ask the students to experiment in groups, and to decide which approach is the most effective, with the following exercise:

> One student reads Lady Macbeth's lines 15–21. S/he should freeze at every punctuation mark. Other students should, during this freeze, shout out words that express what the character is really thinking. For example: 'All our service', (the last service we will do for you apart from your murder). The word 'double' might lead to thoughts about double the damage that might be done . . .

Ask the students to polish these productions, and to present them to the rest of the class.

Ask the students to read all of Banquo's lines – there aren't many – in 1.3, 1.4, 1.6, 2.1, 2.3, 3.1 and 3.3. What kind of man emerges? Ask the students to compare his character with Macbeth's.

Plenary (5 minutes)

This is an opportunity to reinforce the main issue: dramatic irony.

A pleasant seat

Act 1 Scene 6, lines 1–14

1 Recall Duncan's words about the executed Thane of Cawdor in 1.4: 'There's no art / To find the mind's construction in the face. / He was a gentleman on whom I built / An absolute trust.'

   Do you believe that we can tell what is going on in a person's head from the look on his or her face? Or even judge the person's character? Discuss in groups: think of a prominent politician: does his or her face give away what he or she is thinking? Or is it trying to hide it? This thought comes up again near the end of 1.7. Find it.

2 Draw faces of different kinds of people – weak, strong, kind, cruel, stupid, clever, generous, mean – whatever you like – in the belief that you can judge their character from their faces.

3 Research the nesting habits of house martins, to get a grip on Banquo's image in lines 4–10.

4 Re-write Lady Macbeth's lines in this scene as if she were saying what she really thought about the King. You might use Shakespearean language, or modern. You could use the language of a soap opera.

5 Pick out all the words in lines 1–14 that are to do with friendship, welcome, happiness. Begin with 'pleasant', 'sweetly', 'approve' and 'loved'. There are at least twelve.

6 Read lines 1–14 individually, from the beginning of the scene to Lady Macbeth's first words ('All our service . . .'). Refer back to 1.5 and make notes: what do we, the audience, know that Duncan and Banquo don't know? Share your notes in groups. This knowledge of something that the audience has but which some of the characters don't is 'dramatic irony'. Dramatic irony is always a useful idea to bear in mind when studying any play.

   An example: a play, written in the 1950s, has a group of friends meeting on New Year's Eve 1913, drinking to a 'Happy New Year – may it bring peace!' World War I effectively began six months later: they weren't to know that, but we, the audience, do. That's dramatic irony.

7 Study Lady Macbeth's speech here. Say it aloud and interrupt with 'Fair is foul' every time she says something untrue, or at every line ending and punctuation mark.

8 While one student reads Lady Macbeth's lines, get him or her to stop at every punctuation mark, and suggest what is really in her mind at that point.

5 'Twere well it were done quickly

Act 1 Scene 7, lines 1–28: available online and at the end of this book.

Introduction

This section introduces the soliloquy. Encourage the students to read this one, concentrating on the lines that seem accessible (most of lines 13–24).

Aims

Students will learn the meaning and etymology of the word 'soliloquy', and be able to find other examples in the play. They will understand Macbeth's reluctance to assassinate the King, and how he stands in relation to his wife in this matter. They will reflect on ambition.

Starter (15 minutes)

The etymology of 'soliloquy' often fixes the meaning in students' minds: the word comes from the Latin *solus* (as in our words 'solo' and 'solitary'), and another Latin word *loqui* 'speak' (as in our 'loquacious'). So a soliloquy is a speech spoken by a character on his or her own.

Main phase (40 minutes)

In this soliloquy Macbeth gives himself several reasons for not killing his king. They come in lines 10–28. The key ideas are:

1 justice (and there will be revenge from heaven if Macbeth goes through with his plans)
2 family (the keyword is 'kinsman')
3 loyalty to a king
4 hospitality
5 the king's goodness
6 religion runs like a thread through all of these.

Ask the students to find these reasons.

Point out to the students that, while it would be dreadful to kill a monarch today, to Shakespeare's contemporaries it was an even more wicked crime than we can imagine. A king or queen was God's representative on earth, and practically everybody believed in God (and a Hell where you would end up for your sins – especially regicide). To kill a king was close to killing a god.

Hospitality was also seen as a much stronger duty than it is now. Ask the students to study lines 10 to the end, first individually, and then in pairs. Ask them to imagine that they have been asked to write a version of the play in modern language. They must give each of Macbeth's reasons for not killing Duncan in language that would be easily understood today. Lines 13–14 might read, for example, 'I am a cousin / uncle, and he is a guest in my house: both of these are good reasons against killing him . . .' This activity should be done in groups.

Ask the students to find the only reason Macbeth cites in favour of the assassination, which comes in lines after those given online: an idea obviously central to the play.

Groups should share their modern versions of Macbeth's soliloquy, and perform the speech, swapping speakers at each punctuation mark.

Plenary (5 minutes)

Finally, introduce the idea of the euphemism, and offer some: 'pass away' for 'die', for example. Ask them to find Macbeth's euphemisms for murder in this speech: 'it', 'surcease', 'deed' are three.

Glossary

Surcease: an act bringing about an ending.
Trammel: catch, as in a net.

'Twere well it were done quickly

Act 1 Scene 7, lines 1–28

1   Do you ever talk to yourself? Or think about what has happened or what you might do next? Either way you were making a soliloquy. Before you study this one, find other soliloquies in the play. Macbeth has one in 2.1 and another at 3.1 – and there are others.

2   Study the first seven lines of the soliloquy. The broad sense is this: 'If there were no consequences resulting from the murder, I'd do it and not worry about what's to come'.

3   Study lines 10–25 of this soliloquy. Work through it in pairs, and decide what reasons Macbeth thinks of for not killing the King. Act it together, changing speaker at each reason, or speaking each reason in a different voice.
    * Discuss: what seems to be the strongest reason not to kill the king to you?
    * What seems to be the weakest reason?

4   Imagine that you have been asked to write a version of *Macbeth* in modern language. In pairs or individually, write a version of this soliloquy that would be understood on *EastEnders* or *Coronation Street*. You might begin like this:

> I mean, he is my own brother. He's the boss of our family, always has been. That goes for a lot with us. And he's in my house! It's my job to lock the doors to protect him.

5   Hotseat Macbeth. One student sits in the middle of the room. He or she must answer honestly as Macbeth. The rest ask him questions. You might begin with:
    * What was your state of mind when you left the field of battle? When you left the witches?
    * Would you have gone on with this murder if it weren't for your wife?
    * Do you believe in Hell as a place of punishment? Will you go there?

6   What sort of man was Duncan? Describe his character, using his appearances and what others, especially Macbeth, say about him.

7   Write a soliloquy in which you debate with yourself a decision you have to make: whether to stay in or go out, whether to agree to a date or not.

8   If you have already studied *A Midsummer Night's Dream*, go back and quickly find a soliloquy there.

9   'Vaulting ambition which o'erleaps itself' (line 27): make a cartoon to illustrate this image, and another to illustrate 'pity, like a naked newborn babe / Striding the blast'.

I have given suck

Act 1 Scene 7, lines 35–41, 46 and 48–59: available online and at the end of this book.

Introduction

A display of images of babies alongside images of modern warfare will graphically emphasise how babies – and children in general – signify innocence and vulnerability in this play.

Children are also important for another reason: they signify the continuation of a family line and, as Macduff points out later in the play at a terrible moment for him (4.3), Macbeth has no children. The students are to find this reason for the importance of children on the worksheet.

The relationship between the Macbeths will only be partly understood without some discussion of the sexual element of Lady Macbeth's taunting of her husband.

Aims

The students will appreciate how important images of babies and children are in this play, and how they are contrasted with military violence. They will develop a further understanding of Lady Macbeth's role in egging her husband on to the assassination.

In the lines from 'Was the hope drunk' to 'desire', the students will see how she taunts Macbeth: she contrasts his failure to be resolute with his sexual desire ('To be the same in thine own act and valour / As thou art in desire . . .').

Starter (10 minutes)

Ask the students to brainstorm all the words that they associate with babies. You might begin with 'vulnerable', which might lead to 'wobbly', 'tiny', 'immobile'. Words about bodily functions will come up, especially from students who have looked after young siblings: these words can be used to emphasise babies' dependence on adults. Now ask them to brainstorm all the adjectives that come to mind, when they read these lines, to describe Lady Macbeth.

Main phase (40 minutes)

With a group of students taking each act, ask them to scour the whole play for all references not only to babies, but to older children. Here are some examples: at 1.3, line 65, one of the weird sisters tells us that Banquo shall 'get' ('father') kings: his sons. Later in the scene, Macbeth mentions this prophecy twice: it clearly troubles him. In 1.5, Lady Macbeth's words about milk are about children. The lines in this scene stand out. Macbeth mentions 'men-children' later (line 73). And a child appears in other places, including 3.3 and 4.1. One appears, only to disappear, in 4.2.

Ask the students to share their discoveries, and to write a quick note about some of the children mentioned: Macduff's 'pretty chickens and their dam / [killed] At one fell swoop . . .', for example, in 4.3.

Ask them to act lines 35–41 and 47–54 (Lady Macbeth's words from 'Was the hope drunk' to 'desire' and from 'What beast' to 'unmake you'. One student is Macbeth, and sits in the middle of the room. Everyone else is Lady Macbeth. These students walk round Macbeth, shouting the speech at him, handing over to another speaker at each punctuation mark. Repeat with different students acting Macbeth.

Plenary (10 minutes)

Discuss how it felt to be Macbeth in the last exercise. Discuss as a whole class ways of rewriting the taunting lines in modern speech.

I have given suck

Act 1 Scene 7, lines 35–41, 46 and 48–59

1 'The cat in the adage' (or proverb) wanted fish – but was, like all cats, scared of the
   water. Lady Macbeth says that her husband is like that: he wants the crown but is scared
   because of all the reasons he gave in his soliloquy. Make up your own adage in a small verse,
   like this:

> The man wanted glory in the match
> But hadn't the bottle for the hard tackle.
>
> The dancer wanted to be great
> But hated the pain of practice.

2 Write up the lines in which Lady Macbeth taunts her husband, but in language that would
   suit a modern soap opera:

> Is that hope you had still smashed?
> Does it feel like throwing up to look on what was so good before?

3 Babies haunt this play. We see one in Lady Macbeth's speech above. Its life, you could say, lasts
   some twenty-five words. Write a poem in three lines that is a description of that life.
   Here is an example:

> She smiled in my face.
> If I'd had words, before she unbrained me,
> I would have called it love.

4 In groups, each taking an act, find all the references to babies.
   - Why do you think babies are important in this play? Make up possible reasons individually,
     and then share them in groups.
   - Why do babies matter to us today? Are there other reasons, now not so important, why they
     mattered more in Macbeth's time, and to people of Macbeth's high status?

5 Read the lines from 'I have given suck' to 'face' and underline or note down all the words that
   we might associate with a womanly response to a baby. Or a humane, or decent, response.
   Recall, if you can, your first sight of a newborn baby sister or brother, or cousin: write down
   what your first reactions were. Now read the lines from 'Have plucked' to the end of the
   speech. Read the lines aloud, shouting the words that are the most shocking, the most, we
   might say, unwomanly or unmotherly.
   Or is the very idea of an 'unmotherly' woman sexist?

6 In groups, work up ways of saying these lines with a contrast between the first part, which
   contains the words 'given suck', 'tender', 'love' and 'smiling', and the second part, which has
   very different words. Aim to shock your listeners.
   Then, divide the class into pairs, with one student in each pair acting Macbeth, and the
   other acting Lady Macbeth. Act from 'What beast' to 'unmake you'. Lady Macbeth should speak
   contemptuously and Macbeth should react as he sees fit. Each part should be open to male and
   female students.

Here's a knocking indeed

Act 2 Scene 3, lines 1–25: available online and at the end of this book.

Introduction

This is the only comic scene in this play. Discuss the importance of such a scene: it is some relief after the blood, the dagger and the weird sisters. But not much: the porter provides a dark commentary on what is going on in the main action.

Aims

The students will see, first, how the porter supplies much-needed comic relief; and how he comments on the main part of the play. They will understand, not only what equivocation is, but how it is a central theme of this play. They will develop further their understanding of a cluster of related abstract nouns, such as 'contradiction' and 'oxymoron'.

Starter (10 minutes)

Explain equivocation. As so often, the etymology is helpful: it comes from the Latin *aequus* ('equal') and *vox* ('voice'): so equivocation is saying something that can mean different things; it is using ambiguity to deceive.

Act the difficult sentence from 'Faith, here's an equivocator' to 'equivocate to heaven'. The equivocator tells deliberately misleading half-truths ('swear in both the scales against either scale'). The porter's grim joke is that, though the equivocator could play with words to deceive men on earth, it didn't work in heaven.

Main phase (40 minutes)

This next activity could be done in groups, with students parting out the scenes to examine among themselves, and then getting together to share what they have found.

Ask the students to find lines in this scene that have parallels in the rest of the play. There are links to the 'double-speak' of the weird sisters; to lines in the first scene of the play; and to many lines in the rest of Act 1.

They should include in this search all unhelpful answers: when Macbeth, for example, asks the weird sisters 'What are you?' (1.3, line 47) they tell him, not what they are, but what he will be. Ask them to include, too, all apparent contradictions, such as 'Fair is foul'. And include answers that promise good things (the weird sisters' words to Macbeth in 1.3, lines 46–48 and to Banquo lines 63–64). Ask them to note the Old Man's line at the end of 2.4, which encapsulates the whole play: 'That would make good of bad, and friends of foes'.

Ask the students to prepare a presentation of this scene in groups, up to the entry of Macbeth.

Plenary (10 minutes)

Summarise equivocation. A thesaurus offers the following words among many others: 'ambiguity', 'double meaning', 'deviation', 'quibbling'.

Ask the students to listen to politicians speaking on TV or radio to see if they can hear any examples of 'double-speak'. Or: a football manager of a team expected to win 4–0 is facing the press after his team drew 0–0. 'It was good result – we learned a lot from this game'.

Here's a knocking indeed

Act 2 Scene 3, lines 1–25

1. Actors say that it is impossible to act while drunk (though no doubt many have tried). It is difficult, as well, to act being drunk. Taking turns, read, or better say, the porter's speech, or parts of it, as for a radio play, sounding (a) slightly tipsy and (b) roaring drunk.

2. Now act it as if on stage, again either tipsy or extremely drunk. Keep one foot still, and move the other backwards, forwards, then backwards again. Whenever the script has inverted commas – 'i'th'name', 'th'expectation', 'th'other', merge the words: 'ithname' and so on . . .

    Think: what other characteristics do drunk people show when they talk? Often, for example, they over-emphasise some words to try to show that they are not drunk. Put some of these characteristics into your acting.

3. What kind of character is the porter? Read his lines quietly, and with the insights you have gained by acting him, write down some adjectives that would suit him. Give a reference from the scene to back up each adjective. For example, he is irreverent (his words to his superior from line 20 onwards).

4. Imagine yourself as the porter – but later in the day, and after a doze, and now stone cold sober. Write lines for him to say about what happened. Does he regret anything? How well does he remember who it was who knocked? They might begin: 'I don't remember much, but . . .'

5. Prepare, in groups, a presentation of this scene, up to the entry of Macbeth. Make Macduff sound formal, stiffly sober, disapproving of the porter, to supply a sharp contrast to the porter.

6. Scour the play, looking for all the examples of equivocation, or double-speak.

7. Here are two statements of opinion about the porter:

    > This nasty man, with his silly jokes about tailors and farmers, and his smut about drink and sex, is an interruption of a great play. He gets in the way . . . I wish Shakespeare had never included him! He's only there to give the actor playing Macbeth time to get out of daywear (end of 2.2) into his nightclothes (2.3.38).

    > I am so glad the Porter is there is Macbeth. Not only is he funny, but he is central to the play's themes. In between all the nightmare we have seen before and which we will see later, the knocking on the door, and the porter's reaction to it, provide a taste of real life.

    Which of these opinions do you feel is closer to your own? Say why. Make your own additions to the debate.

8 Your royal father's murdered

Act 2 Scene 3, lines 89–113: available online and at the end of this book.

Introduction
Here is more dramatic irony, and therefore a chance to reinforce this concept.

Aims
Students will consolidate their understanding of dramatic irony, and study examples of hyperbole. They will appreciate how Shakespeare builds dramatic tension at the heart of a play, and how even the shortest speeches tell us about a character's motives.

Starter (10 minutes)
Revise dramatic irony, referring back to Part 4. In 1.6, the audience knows something that Duncan and Banquo, arriving innocently at the Macbeths' castle, do not. Ask the students to list the facts in this scene that we know – but that Macduff, Malcolm, Lennox and Donalbain don't.

Main phase (40 minutes)
Students should study individually Macbeth's description of Duncan's body (from 'Here lay Duncan' to 'entrance') in the light of what only they and the Macbeths know. Then, in groups, they should act it, taking turns to be all the characters. Point out that it takes a powerful actor to say Macbeth's lines with the phoney sincerity they call for. It might be better to pretend to faint, but that way out is open only to one of the Macbeths! Make sure the students appreciate the nature of the tightrope the Macbeths walk in this scene.

> 'The spring, the head, the fountain of your blood . . .
> . . .
> His silver skin laced with his golden blood . . .'

Ask the students to reflect on these two lines, and to pick out three key words. It's very difficult, of course. Almost every word is key: 'spring'? 'head'? 'fountain'? 'blood'? (this one is a vital word throughout the play). Ask them for words to describe the lines: 'over the top', 'exaggerated', for example. Ask them to examine the phrases 'silver skin' and 'golden blood'. Why does Macbeth talk like this? Is skin ever silver? Or blood golden? Ask the students: What is going on in Macbeth's head here? Is he deranged?

Introduce the idea of 'hyperbole'. It comes from the Greek words for 'throw' and 'beyond'. One pale English word is 'overstatement'.

In this scene, everyone except the Macbeths has some reason to suspect someone else. Sometimes people say in embarrassing situations: 'I didn't know where to look!' Ask the students to act the scene. They should make no eye contact with anyone else. If they do, they look shiftily away. Then, in groups, they should decide: who has most reason to suspect whom?

Plenary (10 minutes)
Go through the cast present in this scene, and summarise the students' findings about the characters' suspicions.

Your royal father's murdered

Act 2 Scene 3, lines 89–113

1 Look at Macbeth's lines from 'His silver skin' to 'gore'. Using pastels or paint, make an abstract design that illustrates the lines. The colours are in Shakespeare's script. Choose shapes that suit the words.

2 Some very short speeches are important here between lines 89 and 125. Examine the shortest, especially those spoken by Macduff (there are three), Malcolm and Lady Macbeth. Which are the most sincere? Here are some questions to help you decide: 'Wherefore [Why] did you so?' asks Macduff, when Macbeth says he has killed the servants. Why does he ask this? And is Lady Macbeth's faint ('Help me hence, ho') genuine?

3 Think hard about these speeches individually. Then discuss these questions in groups. Each group should agree, for each speech, a grade, A to E. A is for a very sincere speech, E is for a very insincere one. Each group must give reasons for its marks.

    For example, Macduff's reply (line 124) to Banquo's call to fight against malice is probably completely sincere: we have no evidence that Macduff is anything but a good man: an A or a B seems fair.

4 Focus on Macbeth's lines. Look up 'hyperbole' in a good dictionary. Speak Macbeth's lines to yourself, and then to a friend. How would you describe the lines comparing Duncan's skin to silver, his blood to gold?

    Be an actor. You know – and the audience knows as well – that these words are about as insincere as it's possible for them to be. But you must do all you can to convince the other characters. How do you achieve these conflicting aims?

5 Hotseat Macbeth. Look at the contrast between Macbeth's overdone language and Macduff's bluntness. In answer to Donalbain's question, Macbeth takes twenty-four words to say what Macduff says in four. What is the truthful answer to Macduff's question in line 100?

    Raise all this when you hotseat Macbeth. Some other questions to ask him might be:
    • What made you change your mind about killing Duncan?
    • What are you going to do about Malcolm, the late king's eldest son?
    • What was golden about the king's blood, and what, exactly, was silver about his skin?

6 Write an account of the murder of Duncan in modern English, drawing first on the Macbeths' conversations in 2.2 and second on what Macbeth says in this scene.

7 Interview Donalbain and Malcolm for the news on TV an hour after this scene. Work out first what questions you would like to ask.

8 Be Macduff's closest friend. Write down what he or she hears Macduff say about the events of the night.

Fly, good Fleance, fly, fly, fly!

Act 3 Scene 3, lines 1–21 (not all) and Act 4 Scene 2, lines 70–83 (not all): available online and at the end of this book.

Introduction

These scenes are typical of two central features of the play. The first is the theme of murder: Duncan, of course, and Banquo; but especially the murder of children. And the second is a stylistic feature that we can see throughout the play: there is a briskness in so many of the speeches, a rapidity of action. When Banquo dies, for example, he has no final meditation on life, just a yell of fury, an urgent instruction to his son so that he may take revenge, and a despairing insult for his killer.

Aims

The students will appreciate how Shakespeare, using verse, moves action along at speed. They will also see an example of the way Shakespeare gives glimpses into a character in dialogue: the conversation between the child and the murderer, for example, in the second passage.

They will see yet another example of a central theme of the play – contradictory ideas – in Lady Macduff's words about the way 'to do harm / Is often laudable, to good sometime / Accounted dangerous folly'.

Starter (10 minutes)

Revise equivocation by recalling earlier lines about fairness and foulness, illness and goodness ('ill' here meaning 'bad', not 'sick'), happiness and unhappiness, 'joys' and 'sorrow'; and also the porter's speech in Act 2 Scene 3.

Point out that, though Lady Macbeth herself is not equivocating, an ignoble politician could use her notion to equivocate. 'It might seem wrong to kill this child, but the security of Scotland depends upon it . . .'

Main phase (40 minutes)

Point out the speed with which it might be possible to act both the scenes on the task sheet.

Ask the students to read the first passage as for a radio play. Suggest they do it quickly, hardly letting one student finish one speech before another begins the next. Point out the rapidity, the quick exchanges, etc.

Point out that in the first passage there are three and a half lines that are not brisk. Ask each group to discuss which lines these are. (The First Murderer's second speech from 'The west' to 'timely inn' reads like a poem.) Ask the students: when they speak the lines, should they try to emphasise the difference, or hide it?

Then ask them to act Banquo's dying speech as suggested on the task sheet. Similarly, they should act the lines from Act 4 Scene 2.

Plenary (10 minutes)

Ask the students to notice how characters are shown – the boy's bravery, the murderer's inarticulateness – in the shortest of speeches. The murderer is not just a murderer, but a stupid one, who can think of no better insult than jibe at the boy's childhood. What comes out of the boy's character in lines, short and few as they are? His insults are more inventive; he is defiant and brave.

Point out that the boy's insult refers to the murderer's appearance, the murderer's to the boy's youth. Ask the students to write insults suitable for any of the following. A thesaurus will help:

* a liar
* an equivocator
* a witch
* a regicide.

Fly, good Fleance, fly, fly, fly!

Act 3 Scene 3, lines 1–21 (not all) and Act 4 Scene 2, lines 70–83 (not all)

1. Make a drawing to illustrate a stage direction in one of these scenes: you might choose 'Enter Banquo and Fleance with a torch'; 'First Murderer strikes out the light'; 'Exit Lady Macduff crying "Murder", pursued by murderers and her son'; 'Enter Murderers'.

2. If you have time in an art room, you might make your drawing a study for a larger scale artwork – a painting, perhaps. It is a chance to use contrasting dark and light, as in a painting by Caravaggio.

The first passage

3. Identify what Banquo says in his dying speech. There is (1) a yell of accusation, (2) an order shouted four times, (3) a final loving naming of his son, (4) another order and (5) (for his last word) an insult.

   In groups of five, act this extract as if for a radio play, bringing out as clearly as possible the tone in which each of the groups of words would be spoken. Begin quietly at 'But who did bid' and, after 'the subject of our watch', build the lines up to a loud, dramatic climax at the last line. Or perhaps you have other ideas.

The second passage

4. 'Fair is foul, and foul is fair'. 'So foul and fair a day I have not seen'. There is another example of contradictory speech in Lady Macduff's lines. Revise what you have learnt in other lessons. Divide the play up between you as members of a group, and find all other similar references.

5. Who is the third murderer? See 3.1, lines 75 onward: there are only two when Macbeth employs them. Suggest reasons why Macbeth has sent a third man. Some performances make him Macbeth himself.

   Or has Shakespeare made a slip? The dictionary-maker and critic Samuel Johnson said that Shakespeare never wrote 'six lines together without a fault'. Is this one of them?

6. None of the speeches quoted above from either passage is longer than three lines. Act them, emphasising this, even to the point of coming in with the beginning of a speech almost before your cue has been said. Vary the loudness of your acting: for example, Lady Macduff might speak the lines beginning 'I hope in no place . . .' in a hiss, and the murderer might interrupt her just before she finishes with a shout: 'He's a traitor'.

7. 'Thou shag-haired villain,' says the boy. 'You egg,' says the murderer. Write insults for someone in the play. The insults must mirror the person they are aimed at. For example, for the Porter: 'Thou staggering swigger!' For Lady Macbeth: 'You blood-slimed hand-wringer'. Or you might invent insults, not for a particular character, but someone guilty of a crime that is central to the play: a tyrant, an equivocator, a child murderer, a usurper.

A loving couple?

Act 1 Scene 7, lines 54–59 and Act 5 Scene 1, lines 27–44: available online and at the end of this book.

Introduction

The relationship at the centre of this play is an intimate one: critics have suggested that the Macbeths are the most loving couple in Shakespeare. Tell the students how Hamlet insults Ophelia: 'Get thee to a nunnery' (brothel). In *A Winter's Tale* Leontes banishes his wife for unfaithfulness; but even though, sixteen years later she turns out to be both innocent and alive, they never speak a word to each other after she returns from the supposed dead.

Macbeth and Lady Macbeth seem almost to be halves of the same human being. But as one descends, the other rises . . . then falls. In the second passage on the task sheet, we see Lady Macbeth obsessed with her crime, and mad. But there is a terrible meaning in her sanity, and she sees all too clearly the enormity of what she has colluded in.

Aims

The students will understand something of the relationship that is central to this play: in particular, how the power balance between Macbeth and Lady Macbeth shifts. They will see how a character almost entirely vicious can inspire, in Shakespeare's hands, pity.

Starter (20 minutes)

Ask the students to find every affectionate remark made by Macbeth to his wife. Half the class should scour Act 1, and the other half Act 3. Relevant lines are in the following places:
- 'my dearest partner' 1.5 (in Macbeth's letter to his wife)
- 'my dearest love' (later in the same scene)
- 'love', 'dear wife' and 'dearest chuck' all in 3.2
- 'sweet remembrancer' 3.4.

Main phase (30 minutes)

Ask the students, in groups, to read the scenes containing those phrases. Suggest that this seems to be a happy marriage . . . but there is something missing. A clue is in 4.3, lines 205–221, especially 218: 'He has no children': the Macbeths are childless. Perhaps a child has died. A Freudian explanation worth airing with the students might be that the couple spent all the energy they might have used fathering, mothering and nourishing children in fulfilling ambition . . . The students will be able to discuss this, with guidance.

Ask the students to reprise 'I have given suck', and to take it in turns to act it. While one student, acting Lady Macbeth, speaks, all the others, as Macbeth, react.

Ask the students to prepare ways of acting 'Yes here's a spot' for a radio play. Ask them, in groups, to make suggestions for each other's performances. At each pause, they should work out what event in the play is in Lady Macbeth's mind.

This could be developed further: make a performance of 'Yes here's a spot'. One actor reads this speech and, at every reference to an earlier scene, another actor speaks the lines from that scene.

Plenary (10 minutes)

'He has no children'. If Macbeth had been a father, what difference would this have made to the plot – to Macduff? To Banquo and his family? To Scotland?

A loving couple?

Act 1 Scene 7, lines 54–59

1 Write a poem or a song lyric beginning with the lines

> The Thane of Fife had a wife.
> Where is she now?

or a version of them. Use words from 4.2. For example:

> The Thane of Fife, he had a wife.
> Where is she now?
> A shag-haired villain killed her.

As your poem or song develops, plunder images from throughout the play and put them in your work.

2 Illustrate your poem or song with suitable images: for example, 'shag-haired villain'.

3 Take turns to be Macbeth and Lady Macbeth. Act the lines in the first extract above. Lady Macbeth should hurl the words at her husband: but remember they must be clear. Assume that Macbeth does love his wife: how does he react at the words 'suck', 'tender', 'milks', (remember that Macbeth, according to his wife, is 'too full o'the milk of human kindness'), 'smiling' and 'dashed the brains'? Write down words that might describe his feelings at these points, and do the exercise again with these notes in mind.

4 In one production, Macbeth hugged his wife protectively when she mentioned their dead child. Individually, write down all possible answers to the question 'What happened to their child?' Or perhaps it wasn't Macbeth's child? Discuss other possibilities.

5 Some writers have said that questions about Lady Macbeth and her possible children are irrelevant: talking about them is foolish, because it is treating her as a real person, instead of an invention.

   What do you think of this argument?

6 All the affectionate words from Macbeth to his wife occur in the first three acts of the play. What happens that brings about the change? Identify the place in the play when the change can first be seen.

7 *Lady Macbeth and Macbeth.* This would be a clumsy name for the play – but in some ways not a bad one. Why? Discuss reasons for and against putting on a production with that title.

8 By 5.1, Lady Macbeth is mad, and by 5.5 she is dead. Take turns to act the lines above. At every punctuation mark, the other students make suggestions about what Lady Macbeth, in her sick mind, is thinking of at that point and, if possible, give a reference. For example, at 'Fie, my lord, fie, a soldier, and afeard?', is she remembering Macbeth's uncertainty in 1.7?

Unmanned in folly

Act 3 Scene 4, lines 44–73 (most of): available online and at the end of this book.

Introduction

Once more we see up close the relationship between the Macbeths. But his defeat approaches, and so does her madness and death.

Aims

Students will once again see the importance of the idea of 'manhood' in this play; they will also begin to see the relationship between the two central characters splinter.

Starter (10 minutes)

Revise 1.7, in which Lady Macbeth challenges her husband about his manhood. The students should act this scene again. Also, revise 3.1, where Macbeth challenges the murderers about their manhood:

> Ay, in the catalogue ye go for men,
> As hounds, and greyhounds, mongrels, spaniels, curs,
> Sloughs, water-rugs, and demi-wolves and clept
> All by the name of dogs.

Ask the students: How might you say this speech as Macbeth? Try saying it with utter contempt, or as if sarcastically asking for information.

Main phase (40 minutes)

In this scene, Lady Macbeth accuses her husband of being 'unmanned in folly'. Once again, ask the students to act the scene, from the entry of the Ghost (line 37) up to the Ghost's exit at line 108. The two central characters should be as close as possible to each other, with the others arranged in a circle all around them.

Ask the students playing the Macbeths to speak in stage whispers: they have to be audible, of course, to an imaginary audience; but the actors playing the thanes must find ways of suggesting, first, that they are desperate to hear the whispered words; secondly, that they don't show this desperation; and thirdly, that they can't hear them. Dramatically, it is vital that they don't hear words that are incriminating.

Ask the students to emphasise every mention of the word 'man' in the whole scene.

How would the students present this scene? In Shakespeare's time, Banquo's ghost appeared on stage. Today, it usually doesn't. In one production, the ghost appeared so gory that there was nervous laughter in the audience: to be avoided! Ask the students to write director's notes in two ways: with and without the Ghost present.

Plenary (10 minutes)

Ask the students: What is your idea of a good man?

Raise a problem: To whom does Macbeth say 'Sweet remembrancer'? I have suggested on the task sheet that it is said to his wife ('sweet'), but the other word surely suggests it could be his old friend Banquo.

Unmanned in folly

Act 3 Scene 4, lines 43–63, 73

1. What is your idea of a good woman? How does Lady Macbeth measure up? Remember 'Unsex me here' . . . Write notes on this, bearing in mind motherhood, career, morality, mental abilities and any other things you think are important.

2. Find Macbeth's soliloquy beginning 'Is this a dagger which I see before me . . .' As in this scene, he was experiencing a hallucination. Write a poem with that famous line for a title, or 'The air-drawn dagger'; the poem could use words from a thesaurus, and fly far away from this play.

3. Three chances for some acting:
   - Are you a man? Study 1.7 and then this scene closely; then, in groups, act 3.4 for a radio play, from the entrance of the ghost to its exit. Emphasise, in any way you think appropriate, the word 'man'.
   - Look at 3.1, lines 75 to the end. Again, note the use of 'man'. Macbeth taunts the murderers as Lady Macbeth taunts him. Think of verbs and adverbs that might suit your radio-acting of Macbeth's speech beginning 'Ay, in the catalogue': 'hissing', 'shouting', 'sneeringly', 'aggressively' (and others). Try them out.
   - Act the first passage again, but this time improvise a performance in the round. Two students act the Macbeths. They must whisper their lines to each other, but Lady Macbeth must raise her voice when including the thanes. They must want to hear the whispers, while not giving away that they do. How will you act that? Note the words that are incriminating; that would, if overheard, give evidence of Macbeth's guilt in the murder of Duncan.
   - Act the lines from the entry of the ghost until Lady Macbeth says, 'Sit, worthy friends'. Arrange a dining table. You will need five or six actors. Emphasise all the respectful terms the lords use. Make the words come fast: there should be no breaks between speeches, especially when one speech ends in the same line where another begins.

4. Remember those loving terms Macbeth used towards his wife – 'My dearest chuck' was one. Find the others again. How many affectionate words do either of them say in this scene? There is one unusual affectionate phrase – please find it – but nothing else. At one point, Lady Macbeth is scornful. Where?

5. List everything that has changed in their lives, beginning with the murder. And now Macbeth has a secret from his wife . . . write a speech for him in Shakespearean language if you can in which he tells his wife about that secret.

Blood . . . blood . . . blood

Act 3 Scene 4, lines 122–132, 136–138: available online and at the end of this book.

Introduction

Mr Irwin, a teacher in Alan Bennett's play *The History Boys*, tells his class, 'If you want to learn about Stalin, study *Henry VIII*'. In this session, it should be possible to link Macbeth, both the play and the character, not only to history, but also to some modern tyrants students will know about from the news. Images of dictators from both history and the present day would provide a useful background to this session.

Aims

The students will begin to see that Shakespeare is indeed a man for all times – not least ours. They will see how central to the play the idea of 'blood' is; how his actions would not look out of place on television screens during reports of tyranny and war.

They will see the last of the Macbeths together, and perceive in one word the change in their relationship.

Starter (10 minutes)

Say to the students: 'If you want to learn about Macbeth, study Hitler. And if you want to learn about Hitler, study Macbeth'.

Ask the students to discuss in groups: What is a dictator? Ask them to come up with a list of words that describe the actions of one. Using a thesaurus, they should find other nouns that mean something similar.

Macduff uses one of these words as he begins his fight with Macbeth. Malcolm uses the same word near the beginning of 4.3. Ask the students to find the word in the mouths of both these characters.

Main phase (45 minutes)

Ask the students: what would a society run by a dictatorial leader look like in the UK today?

Using images of modern dictators – Hitler, Stalin, Pol Pot, Idi Amin – suggest that Macbeth is a model for them. Using books and the internet, they should spend as long as possible in this lesson researching the careers of one of these men. Ask them to find aspects of the life they have chosen that are echoes of something in the play. One example is a spy system – Macbeth has told his wife that he has a 'feed' (paid) man in every house that matters.

Ask them to think of other examples of tyranny. In a headteacher, for example: how would a dictatorial headteacher behave? Does the word have a relevance to bullying?

Ask them to go quickly through the play individually and then in groups, up to the end of Act 3, identifying all the actions of Macbeth that are those of a dictator, beginning with the murder of Duncan.

Plenary (5 minutes)

Talk about the use of the word 'blood', and related words such as 'bloody', 'gory' and 'incarnadine', which, since Shakespeare wrote used it in 2.2, has come to mean not just 'to do with the flesh' but 'bloody'.

Glossary

Augures and understood relations: prophesies, and patterns that have meanings.

Blood . . . blood . . . blood

Act 3 Scene 4, lines 122–132, 136–138

1. 'I am in blood / Stepped in so far that should I wade no more, / Returning were as tedious as to go o'er'. Illustrate this image, preferably with paint.

2. When a country commissions someone to design a flag, it is an attempt to represent that country's qualities, aspirations and values. Thus the many-coloured South African flag represents a 'rainbow nation'. Design a flag for this play. What colours would be the main ones? What emblems (if any – and you can't have more than three) will be on your flag?

3. The word 'blood' is inescapable in this play. One critic has said that the play's colours were red and black: the first for the blood spilt and constantly referred to, the second for the darkness in which most of the action happens (and where the blood is spilt).

   Find every use of the word 'blood', as well as any related words. There are at least eighteen in the first three acts. Learn by heart at least five lines with the word 'blood' in them.

4. Choose a dictator, and research his (it is almost always his) life, searching for similarities to Macbeth's. First write down some of your dictator's characteristics. One thing typical of many such characters is given here in lines 131–132: 'Feed' here means 'paid'.

5. There is an empress who, some argue, was a dictator. Can you find who it might be? Find out something about her.

6. In a line not given here, Macbeth says 'for mine own good / All causes shall give way'. Ponder what this means. Can you say anything positive about anyone who can say such a thing?

   Translate the sentence into modern English, perhaps for a heartless character in a soap opera.

7. 'Maggot-pies, and choughs, and rooks'. Find images of these birds. What do they all have in common?

8. 'I will tomorrow – / And betimes I will – to the weird sisters'. Look up the scene where this happens (3.5) and act it groups. Look back in the play, and find the point where Lady Macbeth first hears about the weird sisters and their news. What does her husband tell her now about the sisters?

9. Lady Macbeth says one significant three-letter word in this scene. Read the line where she calls her husband 'Sir', and then re-read her words to him in 1.7. We never see the pair together again.

Macbeth shall never vanquished be

Act 4 Scene 1, lines 68–94: available online and at the end of this book.

Introduction

Macbeth (though he doesn't know it) has had his last conversation with his wife – on stage, at least, and that is what matters to his audience. He has told her that he is going to the weird sisters, and he does.

Aims

This section will enable students to revise central themes in the play, and it will challenge them to work out how a difficult scene might be staged. It will also present them with a problem of what is called 'political correctness'.

Starter (10 minutes)

Ask the students: what echoes are there in this scene – the whole of it, not just the lines on the worksheet – of earlier scenes? They might mention the following characters and issues:

* The Weird Sisters.
* Babies.
* A related issue is the succession to the crown. Macbeth has no children, Banquo had a son and Macduff has – for a while longer – children.
* Equivocation (the second and third apparitions both equivocate, appearing to give Macbeth good news).
* Blood.

Main phase (45 minutes)

Ask the students to choose one of those themes, and to go through as much of the play as they can – at least one act – making notes of each line and reference. One of the themes must be 'babies'. Then in groups, they should discuss what they have found, and link it to this scene.

Another central theme here is royalty, and there are connections with babies: the succession issue, which was a constant in England.

The contemporary king was James I. It is important for the students to understand how different views of royalty were compared to ours today: the monarch was God's representative on earth, and killing one would be a dreadful crime that would lead, not only to an excruciatingly painful execution, but also to everlasting damnation in Hell.

It is helpful if the students know the following. A small lecture is necessary:

* James I (James VI of Scotland) came to the English throne in 1603 and it is likely that he saw this play in 1606. Banquo had been invented by Ralph Holinshed, Shakespeare's source, to represent the root of the Stuart monarchy, of which James was the latest representative.
* Banquo is presented in a favourable light in the play, possibly to flatter the king. In Shakespeare's source, Banquo is an accomplice to the murder of Duncan. Shakespeare leaves that unfortunate fact out . . .

Plenary (5 minutes)

Equivocation: as this is central to the play, and not easy to understand, revise work done on it in Chapter 7 (Act 2 Scene 3).

Macbeth shall never vanquished be

1. The first apparition is 'an armed head'; the second is 'a bloody child'; the third is 'a child crowned with a tree in his hand'. Imagine that you have been asked by the props department to design these figures: make drawings of them, with notes, to assist in effectively presenting the apparitions. How are they to appear? Are they dolls? Whatever happens, they mustn't make the audience laugh.

2. Write a non-rhyming poem with the line 'Blood will have blood' repeated at the end of each stanza.

3. Write a short essay with one of the following titles: 'Babies in *Macbeth* and what they stand for' or 'Who equivocates in *Macbeth*?' Share your results in pairs, and then re-draft, making use of your partner's work. If you have time, make a final draft together, and submit it to the class as a collaborative paper on the subject.

4. Work with an imaginary producer: what would be a good way of staging these lines? How do the apparitions enter? In one production, they emerged from a trap door in the stage.

   Note: the producer can't ask the audience to imagine them, as he or she could with Banquo's ghost: they have very significant props to hold, and the audience must see those props.

5. This is a play in which families are significant: the Macbeths' childless one is contrasted with the Macduffs' family with 'all my pretty chickens and their dam'. Think, first, and then discuss in groups: what is the significance of that tree in the child's hand?

6. Read the Weird Sisters' speeches at the beginning of this act. You may well have done this task before, but here is an opportunity to make a sophisticated poem based on lines 4–36. It could be a 'hell-broth'; or you could make a 'heaven-broth', full of sweetness and light . . .

7. In one speech, a weird sister says: 'Liver of blaspheming Jew, / . . . / Nose of Turk, and Tartar's lips . . .' All three of these nouns denote non-Christians.

   Imagine you are producing the play. The headteacher and the Chair of Governors walk in to a rehearsal just as the Third Witch, acting brilliantly, says those lines so that they curdle the blood. 'You can't say that!' says the head. 'Certainly you can't', says the Chair of Governors. 'They're racist! Who wrote them?'

   What you do? Stick to your guns and argue for keeping the lines in, ask them why they think you should cut them, or . . . what else?

8. Equivocation

   This word has appeared many times in these notes. To understand what it means is critical to getting a grip on the whole play. In this scene, the apparitions have the biggest equivocations in the story in lines 79–80 and 91–93. Learn the lines by heart.

© Fred Sedgwick, 2011. *Resources for Teaching Shakespeare: 11–16.*

Every sin that has a name

Act 4 Scene 3, lines 57–73: available online and at the end of this book.

Introduction

This scene is long, and it is barren of action. And therefore it's less immediate to students. For once, it needs a summary as given below; though I would ask the students to attempt their own summaries first.

Starter (20 minutes)

Assuming the students have read the scene, summarise it in five sections:

- Lines 1–37. Macduff urges Malcolm to go to Scotland's aid, but Malcolm says he suspects Macduff might betray him to Macbeth.
- Lines 38–113. Malcolm believes in Macduff's honesty and says he has access to English help – but his own sins are worse, even worse, than Macbeth's.
- Lines 114–139. But Malcolm was only testing Macduff! He is ready to invade Scotland.
- Lines 139–161. An interlude: Malcolm tells Macduff about the English king's gift of healing. This presents a picture of kingly behaviour in dramatic contrast to Macbeth's.
- The rest of the scene – lines 162 to the end – are largely about the murder of Macduff's family.

Main phase (35 minutes)

This scene presents problems, both for a producer putting the play on, and for the students. Ask the students to study Malcolm's two speeches on the task sheet.

The first begins with a list of adjectives describing tyrannical behaviour. Ask the students to make sure that they know what each adjective means. They will need to be told that the original meaning of 'luxury' was 'lust'. Ask them to act lines 57–60, with each member of the group speaking one adjective loudly, possibly even shouting, and with long pauses between them.

Point out that it is rather late in the play to find out that Macbeth is 'luxurious'! He has the faults of tyrant, but sexually he has seemed close only to Lady Macbeth. Why does Shakespeare have Malcolm reveal this now? Possible reasons:

- Malcolm knows something about Macbeth that noone else – including the Queen – knows.
- Malcolm is spreading his fire, and in this mood he will say anything bad about Macbeth.
- Shakespeare is contrasting Macbeth with the English king we see in lines 139–161.

Ask the students, in groups, to decide which one is the most likely. Or suggest another one.
Ask the students to write down two lists opposite each other: the one naming the qualities of a tyrant, the other of a good king. Ask them to add to the list with their own ideas.

Plenary (5 minutes)

Point out the contrasts between the two sets of adjectives that dominate these speeches.

Every sin that has a name

Act 4 Scene 3, lines 57–73

1 Compile a list of the virtues that would be evident in a good king or queen in our time; in a good football manager; in a good artist; in a good parent; in a good teacher.

2 Here we have two contrasting lists – one the sins of a bad king, the other the virtues of a good one. Make sure that you know what all these words mean.

 In one speech, Malcolm accuses himself of extreme lustfulness (lines 66–72). What is Macduff's response? Write his lines from 'But fear not yet' to 'dames enough' (69–73) in modern English, as if for a soap opera. You might begin 'Don't worry about that, mate . . .'

3 Go back over the whole play and read Macduff's speeches so far. Write notes about your impression of him as a character, and whether this speech changes that impression.

 Talk about whether lust is really so unimportant a sin: 'fear not yet / To take upon you what is yours'.

4 Later in this scene, there's action at last, not just talk – but it's reported action. Study lines 206–221 individually, and then in threes. Decide: What are the keywords in each line? Discuss how you could act the lines for a radio play – very fast, but also distinctly. The reading has to be dramatic, as a contrast to the previous 200-odd lines. Emphasise the words for his wife and children that Macduff repeats, and note them down afterwards.

5 Suddenly, we find that Macbeth is not just a tyrant. List in modern words his other 'sins'. 'Smacking of every sin / That has a name' refers to the seven deadly sins. What are they?

6 Look back at Chapter 8, where we saw a very short scene, largely made up of short speeches. This scene is very different. Why has Shakespeare written such a long scene?

 Possible reasons – discuss which is the most likely:
 * He realised the play was a fraction short (it is only half the length of *Hamlet*).
 * It had to be a long scene to convey complex motives in Malcolm's mind.
 * It was important to break up the staccato rhythm of the play with a long, slow movement.

7 Go carefully through the whole of 4.3, and work out where:
 * Malcolm says he suspects Macduff might betray him to Macbeth.
 * Malcolm says that he was only testing Macduff.

8 Malcolm has described a wicked king. But there is a good ('virtuous') king here, but seen only through Malcolm's and a doctor's eyes. Find that king, and list all the phrases used about him that tell us of his saintliness.

15

I have lived long enough

Act 5 Scene 3, lines 11–28: available online and at the end of this book.

Introduction
As always with this book, it is important that the students study the whole scene. Throughout this one, Macbeth's mood changes suddenly several times.

Starter (10 minutes)
Point out that many people experience mood changes in moments of stress. Ask for examples when students have felt emotionally changeable and jumpy. Offer an experience of your own.

Macbeth's situation is an extreme one, of course: he has murdered his king and his friend, and he runs his country as a tyrant, spying on everyone who matters and having families murdered at will. Whatever bond he had with his wife is broken.

Main phase (45 minutes)
Ask the students to read lines 1–66 and to note each line where Macbeth's mood seems to change. For example, there is a blustering bravado in his first speech; an almost insane rage in his words to the servant; and depression in the lines that follow 'I have lived long enough'. Defiance returns at line 32: 'I'll fight till from my bones my flesh be hacked'.

Ask the students to share their findings, and then to write down a description of each mood in modern English.

Two pieces of acting:
* First, ask four or five students to act, as for a radio play, Macbeth's first speech, changing speaker at each punctuation mark. This will show the jumpiness of Macbeth's mind at this point in the action. They should work on this until they are satisfied with their production. They might then turn it into a short stage play.
* Then, when they are fairly sure of each mood in this speech, ask them, in groups, to act lines 11–28, again as a radio play.

Lists: Shakespeare often packs lines with lists to great cumulative effect. Ask the students to study the list of good things Macbeth says we might hope for in old age, and the bad things. Then ask them to go back to 4.3, and to revise the places where, first, Malcolm lists Macbeth's faults and, second, where he lists the necessary qualities of a good king.

What do the students hope for or fear in their old age?

Plenary (5 minutes)
The Doctor's last words in this scene (technically a soliloquy) express a view that many of Macbeth's servants must have felt. Ask the students to prepare in groups a two-line soliloquy for the servant for him to say after his exit at line 19, or for Seyton to say at the end of the scene.

Glossary
Sere: withered.

I have lived long enough

Act 5 Scene 3, lines 11–28

1. Draw the servant's fearful face as he reacts to Macbeth's insults. Or draw Macbeth's face as he delivers them. Put the two drawings together on one sheet of paper, and choose lines from this scene that are relevant to your drawings.

   If you have time and resources, use the drawings as sketches for paintings.

2. Lists. You may have been asked about your thoughts about hopes and fears for old age. If you have, make them into two three-line poems. They should be simply lists – but try to make each line as close as you can to ten syllables. An example, but only a beginning:

   > Friends, not many, but as many as I
   > Need. And children, grown-ups now, and then their
   > Children. My grandchildren . . .

   Speak them aloud. What adjustments – in word order, or in the addition or subtraction of words – might you make to make them sound Shakespearean?

   Or: Think of an old person you know and of whom you are fond. Write down what qualities accompany him or her in old age, and make your short list poem about that person.

3. Write your own lists of adjectives to describe one of the following characters: Macbeth, Macduff, Lady Macbeth.

4. Shakespeare's plays are rich in insults. Here Macbeth screams insult after insult at the poor servant. In twos, say them at each other with as much force as you can (loudness is not the only way – hissing can be effective). Notice how Macbeth uses colour – red, black, but mostly pale colours (to match the servant's face): cream, goose-like, whey (this is thin milk).

5. Look at the Doctor's final two lines. Continue his or her speech, describing from this minor character's point of view what has been going on in Macbeth's household. Look back at the Old Man's words in Act 2 Scene 4, especially the lines 'A falcon tow'ring in her pride of place / Was by a mousing owl hawked at and killed'. Try to describe a state of affairs where human and other natural values are turned on their heads.

6. Read the whole of this scene and identify each place where Macbeth's mood changes. Find words for the kind of mood he is in at each point – he is, for example, defiant in this first speech – and, using a thesaurus, find other words that will describe each mood. Write them down.

7. We have seen Macbeth in many moods since the beginning of the play, but his mood has been fairly consistent in each scene. This inconsistency in a single scene is new. Scan the whole play and make quick notes about his mood in each scene. You could make this quicker by parting out acts to different groups – but share your findings.

8. The poor whey-faced servant! Write what he says later to his family or friends about this scene (that is assuming, of course, that he survives the battle).

© Fred Sedgwick, 2011. *Resources for Teaching Shakespeare: 11–16.*

The queen, my lord, is dead

Act 5 Scene 5, lines 15–29, 32–34: available online and at the end of this book.

Introduction

Here are some of Shakespeare's most famous lines. It is important, though, that we do not make them like a Grecian Urn, something to be gazed over, wondered at, admired. The activities in this section are aimed at getting students to engage with the lines, and to make them *theirs*.

Starter (10 minutes)

Ask the students to pick out every word that is about lowness, sadness, even depression. We have seen many moods in *Macbeth*. Ask the students to find one other place in the play where we have seen evidence of depression.

Main phase (35 minutes)

In groups, ask the students for suggested ways of acting these lines. They should experiment in as many ways as they can think of. Here are some suggestions:

- in a group, changing speakers at each punctuation mark
- as a public speech, or even as a sermon
- as a talk on the radio
- very quietly, as a private communication of Macbeth with himself
- changing at points from one way to another
- or he simply could say them (or some of them – which?) to Seyton.

Ask the students to think of adverbs, and say the lines as each adverb dictates: for example, say the lines fearfully, angrily, resignedly, miserably, wildly, religiously, hopelessly, or, given Macbeth's changeability at this stage of the play, mixing some of these . . .

Equivocation again: Ask the students to look at lines 42–43: 'the equivocation of the fiend / That lies in truth'. They should look back at 4.3, lines 162–206. Ross equivocates with Macduff, even letting him believe that his wife is 'well', for 44 lines. Contrast this with the way Seyton tells his news. Collect examples of equivocation from throughout the play: to revise this concept is to get near the heart of the play.

Ask them to break bad news to a friend – his team has lost 6–0; her plane will be delayed by another four hours. Do each in two ways: the first equivocating, or at least 'beating around the bush' ('I hope you've enjoyed that duty-free shop, because you'll have more time to explore it . . .') and the second directly.

Plenary (15 minutes)

A critic once wrote that watching one actor playing Macbeth was like watching 'a potentially great man [committing] suicide of the soul'. Ask the students to identify moments in the play when Macbeth is destroying what makes him a human being. They might, for example, find the moment when he says 'for mine own good / All causes shall give way'.

Glossary

A poor player: a mediocre actor. Shakespeare speaks from experience here. Tradition tells us that he played small parts in his plays: the Ghost in *Hamlet*, for example, and the old man Adam in *As You Like It*.

The queen, my lord, is dead

Act 5 Scene 5, lines 15–29, 32–34

1 Say the lines from 'She should have died hereafter' to 'signifying nothing' in all the
ways your teacher suggests.

Collect adverbs to do with misery (or whatever mood you think Macbeth is in at this
moment) from a thesaurus: Here are some to start with:

Glumly, despairingly, mournfully, stoically . . .

Now in groups, find more ways to speak the lines. Imagine different contexts. Speak them:
* as a king talking to his people on the radio
* as a man talking to his priest in the confessional
* confidingly, as to Seyton.

'Dark, hungry, haunted'. That is how one critic described a performance he admired. Ask the
students to find a moment in the play when each of those adjectives seen exactly right. There
could be more than one moment for each adjective, of course.

2 Equivocation again! Revise what we mean by this word in the following ways: tell each other
in groups of two or three what you understand by the word; go through this book and study
again three examples in the play; look it up in a dictionary or a thesaurus.

Now look at line 42. Here Macbeth says he 'begin[s] / To doubt th'equivocation of the fiend'.
Which fiend does Macbeth refer to? Which equivocation is he referring to? It's in one of the
scenes with the weird sisters. Revise those scenes.

3 Seyton seems to get off better at his master's hands than the messengers: perhaps he is closer
to the king. Write down his words to his wife/best friend when he tells them about Macbeth's
behaviour. Do it in Shakespearean style.

Or: be old Seyton, and reminisce about these long gone days – the death of the queen,
Macbeth's reaction, how he treated the servants, how he reacted to the messenger's news about
the moving wood.

4 Learn one of the following speeches in the play by heart: Lady Macbeth's lines in 1.5
beginning 'Glamis thou art'; her lines in the same scene beginning 'The raven'; her lines in
1.7 beginning 'I have given suck'; the porter's first speech in 2.3; Macduff's lines in the same
scene beginning 'Awake, awake!'; the whole of 3.3 from 'A light!' to the end; Lady Macbeth's
sleep-walking lines in 5.1; or the lines in this scene beginning 'Tomorrow' and ending with
'nothing'. Note down what each speech tells us about the character/s who speak them.

5 Write a mini-saga of the story of the play. It should have no more than fifty words – and, if
possible, exactly that. You will find that, by trying to keep to a strict limit, you will discover
what to you are the most important elements in the play, and what is less important.

Section 2   *A Midsummer Night's Dream*

17

Our nuptial hour

1 Act 1 Scene 1 lines 1–19: available online and at the end of this book.

Introduction

The early scenes of Shakespeare's plays almost always give us clues about what's to come, and students should be trained from the beginning of their studies to examine them. Certain themes emerge quickly in *A Midsummer Night's Dream*.

Aims

To help the students to understand how Shakespeare does this. Themes include: discord in families, the moon and 'the course of true love'.

Starter (10 minutes)

Briefly mention the place of Theseus and Hyppolita in Greek mythology: Theseus, Duke of Athens, had fought against a warlike tribe of women called the Amazons. He had won, and taken their leader, Hyppolita, captive.

Main phase (45 minutes)

Discuss: a marriage that has begun in war . . . does the stilted language between them here tell us something about their relationship? In one production Theseus was a grey-beard still in armour, so formal that his line to Philostrate (12–13) about stirring up youth to merriment was met with laughter from the audience.

Ask the students to prepare in pairs a performance of the first eleven lines of the play. They should practise reading the lines in different ways, and then present their version in the way that seems best.

Some suggestions. All seem feasible except the first and the last, but they are worth trying:

- Theseus arrogant, Hyppolyta subservient and flirtatious
- Theseus arrogant, Hyppolyta defiant
- both simply stately; they hardly know each other
- Theseus nervous, Hyppolyta confident
- they might try to read the scene as sincere lovers.

Ask the students to count mentions of the moon from lines 1 to 110. Ask them to discuss in groups, first, what the moon stands for in our culture, and, second, how differently we understand the moon from the way Shakespeare's contemporaries must have understood it. We see it, for example, less mysteriously.

- It stands for love.
- It stands for madness: the Latin name for the moon is Luna; hence, of course, 'lunatic'.
- It stands for the woman's monthly cycle.

Point out that Hyppolita composes a short poem about the moon: 'The moon, like to a silver bow / New bent in heaven'. Ask the students to write a similar poem of no more than twenty words with a strong simile like this one about any heavenly body: 'And now the comet, like a gowned visitor / come from afar'.

Plenary (5 minutes)

Talk about discord in families, starting with relatively minor disputes in your own: what to have for dinner, where to go on holiday. Discuss other subjects that cause disagreement. Ask the students to watch out for examples of quarrels within families and within friendships in this play.

Our nuptial hour

Act 1 Scene 1, lines 1–19

1. The moon is a silent character in this scene up until line 110. Re-read Hyppolita's first speech, and make a quick drawing to illustrate her metaphor ('like to a silver bow'). Then write a moon poem, or a star, or sun, or planet poem with a simile.

2. Read the rest of this scene, noting down examples of discord and the course of true love running less than smoothly. Who argues with whom? About what?

3. Choose one act of the play, and make a note of every mention of the moon, and who it is who mentions it; and memorise every line with the moon (or 'moonshine' or 'moonlight') in it.

4. Discuss in groups: What does the moon stand for?

5. Discord. This marriage between Theseus and Hyppolita seems to be about to start in a strange way: look at that stilted language, and listen to Hyppolita's words over the next hundred lines. How many are there? – none: silence for over a hundred lines. Choose one speech, and make notes about what she might be thinking.

   In one production, Hyppolita gave Theseus a good slap in the middle of line 122 between 'Hyppolita' and 'what cheer' when he told Hermia that she must marry Demetrius.

   In groups, arrange for two students to act lines 1–11 for a radio play. Always bear in mind with Shakespeare's plays (and in all plays from this period) that actors were male. Young men or boys acted the women's parts. Today anyone may take any part the director chooses. It can be revealing when a male actor plays a woman, and vice versa.

6. Egeus has a long speech here. Arrange for students to play the other characters present, reacting to what the old man says. Then, each student should rehearse ways of saying it:
   * The actor playing Egeus should look at each character he is addressing.
   * He should change tone of voice and posture at every question mark.
   * What moods do you want to show? Anger, resentment . . .

   It's clear that Egeus thinks very little of Lysander: look at the list of presents he has seen his daughter receive from him: 'bracelets of thy hair, rings, gauds, conceits, / Knacks, trifles, nose-gays, sweetmeats . . .' (lines 33–34). 'Gaud' comes from the same source as our word 'gaudy': it means a flashy, worthless trinket. Write a list of presents that Egeus might see as representing a more sincere love; or that you yourself might see as representing the real thing.

7. Write a speech for a soap opera today. A parent doesn't approve of a son/daughter's choice of partner. Write the parent's lines.

8. Egeus has very few more lines. Here, he sounds a bit boring. How can you make the speech not boring? When you have read the whole play, make a case for (a) cutting this speech out altogether, (b) cutting it down or (c) keeping it in.

18

The raging rocks
and shivering shocks

Act 1 Scene 2, lines 1–15: available online and at the end of this book.

Introduction

The laughs in *Macbeth* are dark, and all gathered in one scene. Here the comedy is almost slapstick.

Aims

In reading and acting 1.1 and 1.2 the students will appreciate something of Shakespeare's range. A scene change, probably done very quickly in Shakespeare's time, takes us from nobility to the common people. They will begin to appreciate what comedy means in Shakespearean terms.

Starter (10 minutes)

Ask the students to identify ways in which this scene (all of it) differs from the previous one. Ask them not to be shy of mentioning obvious differences.

- It is short, and made up entirely of short speeches.
- It is (apart from 'The raging rocks') in prose, not verse.
- It involves low, rather than high, life.
- It is comic, not potentially tragic: no one (in spite of Quince's fear) is in danger of death.
- It is informal, while 1.1, especially at the beginning, is formal.

Point out that 1.1 ends with a long speech, old-fashioned in its tone and diction ('eyne' for 'eyes', for example), and rhyming in couplets. Then in 1.2, we get a five-word speech of such ordinariness that you can hear versions of it in everyday speech today: 'Is all our company here?' ('Is anyone missing?')

Main phase (45 minutes)

Ask the students to identify each character and find a reason why his name suits his trade.

The students will need to be told about Mrs Malaprop, a character in Sheridan's play *The Rivals* (1775), who used what she would have thought of as clever words, but got them wrong: 'She is as headstrong as an allegory on the banks of the Nile'. Bottom has the same problem. He uses the following malapropisms: 'Generally' is a malapropism for 'severally'. In 'Aggravate my voice', the first word is a malapropism, as is the last word in 'Rehearse most obscenely'.

Ask the students to suggest what Bottom means to say, and ask them to make notes of all his wrong usages throughout the play.

Another difference between the last scene and this is that Quince and his friends are characters of Shakespeare's time: they are not from ancient myths, as Theseus and Hyppolita are. This contrast would have been even more apparent to Shakespeare's contemporary audiences.

Explain that the humour here arises entirely out of character: there are no gags. Ask one student to play Quince up to line 33, while you play Bottom, exaggerating the bombastic control-freakery of his character, and perhaps using an exaggerated version of the local speech.

Ask the students to act the lines in groups of six, taking turns with the different characters.

Plenary (5 minutes)

Revise what the students have learned about the characters in this scene. Ask them to identify one theme already identified in 1.1 that is still present in this scene. It is, of course, love.

The raging rocks and shivering shocks

Act 1 Scene 2, lines 1–15

1. Read the whole of this scene, and make a drawing of Bottom the weaver. He could be in modern costume or in Shakespearean, but your drawing must say something about the character's trade. Decide on some adjectives for his personality, and try to suggest those adjectives in your drawing.

   Then write a character sketch of him.

2. A dramatic contrast: one student should read the last five lines of 1.1 in as melodramatic a way as possible, then two other actors should act the first 23 lines in 1.2.

3. Write down in a left-hand column the names of each of the characters in this scene. In another write his job. In a third, give a reason (or reasons) why his name suits him. For example:

SNUG	joiner/furniture-maker	All the joints in a chair or a table have to fit well, or snugly

4. Look at Bottom's first line. We are told straightaway something central about his character. Now read all his lines to the end of the scene. Write notes about what he is like; mix them with the ideas you have had in section 1 above.

5. These characters are not educated. Make a list of all the silly things they say in this scene and (especially with Bottom) all the idle boasts. Does he really know this play as he tells the others in line 11? And Quince gets confused right at the beginning, before Bottom has rattled him even further: 'His wedding day at night'.

6. Look at the occasions early in the scene when Quince finishes a speech. Bottom puts him right, or offers advice, or comments unnecessarily. Imagine you are Mrs Quince, and write down what your husband says to you about the meeting – especially as it involves Bottom. Do it in language that would suit a soap opera. Begin: 'I've had it up here with that beggar Bottom . . .'

7. This scene is in prose – except for eight lines of verse that are not as 'lofty' (noble) as Bottom thinks. In groups, find ways of speaking the lines beginning 'The raging rocks' that expose how bad they are.

8. When you have studied this scene, read Act 3 Scene 1, lines 1–55. Bottom's character becomes even clearer here.

9. Look at Quince's second speech. He seems sure they will perform the play. Now look at 5.1, lines 44 onwards: it seems the matter is still to be decided. Does this matter? Has Shakespeare made a mistake?

19

With thy brawls thou hast disturbed our sport

Act 2 Scene 1, 88–102: available online and at the end of this book.

Introduction
After the brief speeches of 1.2, Titania's great lines about natural disaster can look forbidding to inexperienced readers. The rest of this section aims to present suggestions for students of all abilities to get inside it, to make it, to a greater or lesser extent, their own.

Images from the media on climate change, storms, tornadoes, rapid cloud movements and the like would make a helpful display here, both as images relevant to Titania's lines, and as a background to some of the students' writing displayed.

Aims
To help the students get to know a sustained piece of verse in iambic pentameters; to get some idea of what an iambic pentameter is; and to reinforce in their minds the notion of discord.

Starter (5 minutes)
Ask the students, working in groups, to pick out from the lines on the task sheet and the rest of the speech any words or phrases to do with discord in nature. For example: brawl, disturbed, revenge, overborne, murrion, diseases, etc.

Main phase (45 minutes)
Now ask the students to look back at 1.1, lines 1–110 for more words that concern discord – ask them to jot down quickly, a list of words about discord, from this speech, mixed up with words about discord from the earlier scene. Include all insults traded. Ask them to jot down, quickly, a list of the words about discord from this speech in a random way (any old how) mixed up with the discordant words from the earlier scene.

Ask them to write a poem, addressing a real or imaginary human, with insults. Examples are Lysander's line (1.1.110): they might begin with 'You spotted and inconstant man'.

Introduce the idea of the iambic pentameter. Ask the students to count the syllables in each line from 88 to 91. There are ten in each line. Each te-TUM is called a foot, and there are five feet in each line, hence PENTameter, as in PENTagon. The metre of each line is like this:

Te-TUM-te-TUM-te-TUM-te-TUM-te-TUM.

Or you could put it like this:

.- .- .- .- .-

so the first syllable is unaccented.

Point out that each line can be read in this way. Then show them how Shakespeare is not as monotonous as that.

Plenary (10 minutes)
It is not difficult to compose bad iambics. Suggest some, emphasising heavily the second syllable of each foot:

In <u>dreams</u> the <u>cats</u> go <u>searching</u> <u>in</u> the <u>bins</u>.

Ask the students: Can you think up a bad iambic pentameter?

With thy brawls thou hast disturbed our sport

Act 2 Scene 1, 88–102

1   Make a drawing of one of the examples of extreme weather described in this speech.
    Two suggestions:

> 'the winds . . . / . . . have sucked up from the sea / Contagious fogs'
> 'crows are fatted with the murrain flock'.

Now write Titania's line in – not necessarily under – the drawing: make the line an integral part of the art work.

   If you have time and resources, make a painting based on your drawing.

2   Read Titania's speech – first just the part online, but later, the whole speech – making notes or underlining all words or lines that are not immediately easy to understand.

Some words are obsolete today:
- 'Murrion' means diseased; 'nine-men's-morris' was a board game like draughts which could be played on a piece of land with men pretending to be the pieces.
- Some lines can be worked out: 'the beached margent of the sea', for example. Similarly, 'ring-lets' and 'the pelting river'.
- The ox 'stretching his yoke in vain', and the ploughman 'losing his sweat'; the 'green corn / rotted ere he attained a beard' – these might require some thought (though probably not if you live in a farming community).

Individually, work out your sense of these lines. Then pool your thoughts in groups, and come to an agreed decision about what they mean.

3   Climate change
    Make a manga – a cartoon book – for any group of lines in this speech, writing the relevant line/s under each image.

4   Who is the boss? In line 61 of this scene, Titania prepares to leave, but Oberon orders her to stay. 'Am I not thy lord?' And Titania can only obey: 'Then I must be thy lady'.

   Where else in the play so far have men made their power to dominate women clear? In Shakespeare's time, the male dominance over the female was simply accepted. Today this is, to say the least, questionable. Act out lines 60–64. Take turns as Titania: does she make it clear that, although she will stay, she does so only because she must?

   Take one scene, and find more examples of discord in the rest of the play.

5   Write an iambic pentameter, as silly as you like. Here's one:

      When Jim goes down the path I like his tread.
      The rhythm is like this:
      Te-TUM-teTUM-te-TUM-te-TUM-te-TUM
      .- .- .- .- .-

6   'No night is now with hymn or carol blessed.'
    What a sad line that is! Write a poem where each line has ten syllables. Replaces 'hymn', 'carol' and 'blessed' with words of your choice. Make your lines as close to iambic pentameters as you can.

20

I'll follow you

Act 3 Scene 1, lines 83–93: available online and at the end of this book.

Introduction
A recording of Sting's song 'Every breath you take' will set the mood here. Puck, like the singer, is threatening to be a stalker.

Aims
The students will understand something of the characters of the mechanicals, of Puck, and of Titania. They will have an opportunity to put part of the play on. They will glimpse some of Shakespeare's inspiration in Ovid's poem *Metamorphoses*, and what it taught him about change.

Starter (5 minutes)
Revise the context of this speech: Puck has just dropped the love potion in Titania's eyes; now the mechanicals – Quince and the other Athenian workmen – have turned up to rehearse their play.

Ask the students to listen to Sting's song: they might look at the lyric. Ask them to compare the lyric to Puck's lines.

Main Phase (45 minutes)
Change is central to this play: remind the students of the climatic changes that Titania has described. Shakespeare had read the first-century Latin poet Ovid whose great poem *Metamorphoses* is all about change: a woman is transformed into a bird, stones become people, a girl becomes a laurel tree. Ted Hughes' book *Tales from Ovid* is a powerful and accessible version of this poem.

Lead some discussion about change – in flora and fauna, in the seasons, in decay; in human life, as seen in families; in the lives of machines; in fashion; in technology. The following simple formula facilitates thinking on this subject:

> I used to _____
> But now I _____
> And soon I will _____

In discussion, ask the students to come up with little stanzas with that pattern – first about their own lives, and then about something outside themselves. A student wrote:

> Once I was a dribbling stream on a hill
> But now I am a wide river you can't cross
> And soon I will be the vast sea.

There are other less prominent examples of change in the play. Even though Hermia and Lysander end up together, the death-threats of Theseus and Egeus are put aside; Titania's love for her Indian boy seems to fade, and neither is Oberon bothered about him; Titania is changeable in her 'doting' on Bottom; and Oberon's potions encapsulate romantic changes.

In 1.2, Quince and his friends assume that they are to put on their play; by 5.1, we learn it is still an open question.

Raise the question: are some of these changes the result of the pressure Shakespeare was under to get a play ready for the stage? Or are they part of the main theme? These questions should be discussed in groups.

Exit: that stage direction hides much action. Ask the students to picture, and then act, the mechanical leaving in terror.

Plenary (10 minutes)
Suggest that the students share their verses written in the pattern above.

I'll follow you

Act 3 Scene 1, lines 83–93

1. Observe changes: in people, in clouds, in animals . . . and write notes about them.
   Or: Write a poem beginning with the line 'Change and decay in all around I see'.

2. Puck is one of those characters that can be acted in many different ways. There have been cockney Pucks, elderly Pucks, country bumpkin Pucks, Pucks whose evil side dominates, Pucks who are more naughty or mischievous than wicked. There have been female Pucks. In groups, decide on different ways of saying the lines beginning 'I'll follow you . . .'.
   One version should be threatening: the lines of a stalker. Vary the loudness of your voices: hissing some lines, and shouting others.

3. Bottom is changed in this scene. The men lovers Lysander and Demetrius change in their affections. Theseus has changed from being Hyppolita's enemy to being her husband. Can you find other examples of change in the play? Make notes about as many as you can find.
   Change is very important here. Write a poem or a short prose account about some change that you have witnessed:
   * a puppy or a kitten changing into a mature cat or dog
   * a baby sister or brother growing up
   * trees and plants changing as the seasons change.

4. Shakespeare has set this speech in an Athenian wood. Or has he? The mechanicals – the clowns – make it feel like an English setting. We can do what we like with this speech, so write a speech about following someone, or even stalking them. Prepositions and prepositional phrases are valuable here: before, about, within, between, over, under, in front of, in the middle of, and set the speech anywhere you like.
   One musical student set his speech in the orchestra, and wrote this:

   > I'll follow you
   > Between the percussion instruments
   > And deafen you with the tympani
   > And destroy your heartbeat
   > With side drums knocking . . .

5. In groups of six, discuss all the characters who speak in lines 60–118. For example, Flute is young (he only just has a beard coming, remember), and he is not very bright (he never pronounces 'Ninus' right – this is a running gag throughout the play). Quince is (understandably) impatient. One person should write down the findings of the group.

6. Next, design a performance of these lines on an improvised stage. That stage direction, *Exit*, is very blunt. In one production, Quince kept leaving the stage and then coming back fearfully before leaving again; Flute hid behind a tree. Extend your direction to include comic business for all the mechanicals.

21

Doting in idolatry

Various short passages throughout the play: available online and at the end of this book.

Introduction

One of the keywords in *A Midsummer Night's Dream* is 'dote'. Frank Kermode, in his book *Shakespeare's Language*, counts eight uses of it (including 'doting'). This is a high count, when one reads (in Kermode again) that the word appears in no other play more than once. Another keyword is 'eye', with its variations, 'eyes' and the archaic 'eyne'.

Aims

To help the students to appreciate that a key theme here is the opposition between 'doting' ('the work of the eye only' Kermode says) and the 'loving' (the work of the whole mind).

Starter (5 minutes)

Ask the students 'What does the word 'dote' mean?' Ask them, first, to think about it individually; then to pool their ideas in groups, and, finally, to look it up in a dictionary. Ask them also to look up 'dotage'.

Etymology is helpful here. The history of the verb is something like this: 1200 – 'behave foolishly'; 1477 – 'be foolishly fond'; by 1380 – the noun 'dotage', 'foolish behaviour', with the sense of senility around the same time. It is important that students distinguish between 'love' on the one hand and 'dote' on the other.

Main phase (45 minutes)

Ask the students to look back at what Lysander says to Hermia at line 1.1.179: 'Keep promise, love'. Now ask them to read Demetrius' lines from 3.2, 137–144, which begin 'O Helen, goddess, nymph, perfect, divine!' He has just woken, having had the love juice put in his eyes – and he sees the formerly despised Helena first.

This speech is, at least in part, a satirical riff on outdated views of the ideal woman's beauty and the poetry that was written to celebrate it: women had to be fair, red-lipped, pale. See Sonnet 130 for a powerful attack on this kind of writing.

Ask the students, in groups, to prepare performances of this speech that bring out its falseness, its insincerity. Who can sound the most gushing?

Suggest that this is 'doting'. Now ask the students to look quickly through the play from the beginning to the end of Act 3. Only two characters are to be completely trusted in love. Only two are constant to their love at the beginning of the play, and stay constant with no falling away. Who are they? Ask the students to produce evidence for their opinions.

Lines they might suggest are Hermia's declaration to Lysander (1.1.169ff); and Helena's faithfulness to her love for Demetrius, even when appealed to by Lysander in 3.2.

Plenary (10 minutes)

Sum up: What other loves are there in this play that sound unhealthy at times? Titania's doting on her changeling boy fades. Ask the students to think about Oberon's behaviour, and Theseus' words at the beginning of the play. How much evidence is there that Hyppolita loves Theseus?

Doting in idolatry

Various short passages throughout the play

1   Write sentences that begin 'I love . . .' (about friends and family perhaps) and others that begin 'I dote on . . .'. (I dote, for example, on my pet hamster, or on chips with fish, or on 'some idle gaud' from my childhood.)

2   The word 'dote' comes up many times in *A Midsummer Night's Dream*. Using a good dictionary, find out what its possible meanings are, and check, too, on the word 'dotage'.

    Also, in *Romeo and Juliet*, you will find a character, Friar Lawrence, who distinguishes between doting and loving.

3   Act Titania's words above. Remember, first, that she is talking to a donkey, and second, that she has had the love potion poured in her eyes by Puck.

    Should you try to make the audience laugh? Or feel sorry for Titania's situation? Or – if possible – both?

    Note especially the lines about the honeysuckle and the elm: Shakespeare has used the plant and the tree for a subtle erotic purpose.

4   Act Demetrius's words to Helena. Imagine yourself one of the less pleasant male characters in a soap opera, slightly drunk (though don't slur your words) and speak them to a sober woman who wants to be anywhere – but *anywhere* – else.

    Do this in groups, and see who can sound the most 'fulsome' – that is 'cloying . . . disgusting by excess'.

5   Helena's reply to all this falsity is strong: 'O spite! O Hell!' Write your own response to this kind of over-the-top language. One student wrote:

> You cannot take me in by these false lies.
> Why is it you only love me now, not then?
> If you think I am so stupid to believe those lies
> You can think again.

6   Or write your own over-the-top love poem. Another student wrote:

> Oh dear beloved, your hair is darker
> Than the night sky. Your lips are redder than
> Blood. Your face is so beautiful
> It makes the sun look black and the flowers ugly.
> You are more precious than crystals
> And more worthy than gold . . .

7   Two characters are constant in their love in this play. Who are they? How do we know what their attitudes are to love from their words and their behaviour throughout the play?

8   Check out the meaning of the term 'hyperbole'. Find examples of it in the passages on line.

22

My mistress with a monster is in love

Act 3 Scene 2, lines 6–26 (most of): available online and at the end of this book.

Introduction

In most productions of the play, Bottom's 'affair' with Titania is viewed as unproblematical, both from the audience's point of view, and from Oberon's. Students might raise questions about the relationship between king and queen fairy that Oberon's behaviour implies ('Wake while some vile thing is near!' Oberon says at 2.2.40).

Or . . . is this just a comedy we mustn't take too seriously?

Aims

Other aims are to help the students to understand more of the characters of Oberon and Puck, to help them to appreciate Shakespeare's use of extended metaphors, and to examine more examples of the way Shakespeare uses iambic pentameter.

Starter (5 minutes)

Ask the students to discuss how they would feel if their best friend or girl/boyfriend dropped them for someone else. How does Oberon take the news? (line 35).

Main phase (45 minutes)

Ask the students to scour the play so far and find everything that Oberon has said and make notes about his character. For example: Act 2 Scene1: 'Ill met by moonlight, proud Titania!'

He is very much a king, commanding: see also his next line, which is an order: 'Tarry, rash wanton!' Note that 'wanton' had, from Middle English times, suggestions of looseness in morals: Oberon uses strong language.

Act 2 Scene 1 again. Speech beginning 'That very time I saw . . .'. He sees things Puck can't see; he knows about magic. Here and in 2:3 ('I know a bank . . .') he not only talks in blank verse, but in what is clearly poetry: see his use of the names of wild flowers.

Ask the students to make notes about what they have found, and to share them in groups.

Ask them to look back to 2.2.40: 'Wake while some vile thing is near!' What can Oberon have in mind?

And line 35 here.

Ask the students if they can imagine a situation from a soap opera in which someone causes their partner to fall for someone else. What might take the place of Oberon's potion? Drink? Drugs? Ask them to write some dialogue between characters in this situation from a soap opera.

Plenary (10 minutes)

Revise the work done on iambic pentameters. Ask the students to read, in groups, the extracts from Puck's speech given online here. They should change speaker at the end of each line.

First, they should do this reading emphasising the iambic beat; then, a second time, they should bear this beat in mind, but read the line more for the sense. For example, the first time they might read:

> My MIStress WITH a MONster IS in LOVE
> But the second time the line may go
> My MIStress with a MONSter is in LOVE

They should do the same with other lines.

My mistress with a monster is in love

1 Make two drawings of lines 19–31, side by side: one of the birds 'rising and cawing
   . . . madly sweep[ing] the sky', one of the mechanicals' actions in lines 25 onwards:
   ask them to write a short poem with a comparison like this, perhaps of children on a
   primary school playground scurrying about before the whistle blows.

2 In groups, one student reads the lines from 'A crew of patches' to 'Pyramus translated there'
   while the others mime some of his lines.

3 What sort of character is Puck? In groups, go through the play so far, reading all of Puck's
   speeches. Make notes about the personality that emerges from your reading.

4 Even more important, what sort of character is Oberon? Puck tells him 'My mistress with a
   monster is in love', and he replies: 'This falls out better than I could devise'. What does that
   response tell us about him? Write down some adjectives that describe this response.

5 Hotseat Oberon. Here are some questions you might ask him (don't forget that, first, he is a
   king; and second, he has magic powers):
   • What did you think might happen when Puck, on your orders, put the potion into your
     queen's eyes?
   • How did you feel at first about her falling for Bottom?
   • And later?
   • Ask him to talk about how he will feel about her in the future when he remembers this
     adventure.

6 Look at 3.1, lines 174–178. There is a space between this scene and the nest. What happens in
   this gap?

7 Find the moment, later in the play, when Titania wakes from her dream, and note Oberon's
   reaction. Is it reasonable? Discuss this in groups.

8 In twos, act Oberon and Puck in lines 34 and 35. Try different ways. You could leave, for
   example, a long pause after 'ass' while Oberon thinks.

9 Are we at risk of taking this relationship between Titania and Bottom too seriously? It is, after
   all, 'only a comedy . . .'. Think of comedy on television. Can we say of it 'only a comedy . . .'.
   or is it as potentially as important and full of meaning as any other drama? Discuss this in
   groups.

10 More change! Here, for the second time, Bottom is described as having been 'translated'. Find
   all the words in the play to do with change.

23

Helena: a character study

Act 3 Scene 2, lines 198–211: available online and at the end of this book.

Introduction

In this section, students are invited to study one character in the only way possible: by examining her words. Once they have followed the tasks here and on the task sheet, they might do similar studies of the other lovers.

Aims

Students will begin to appreciate the way Shakespeare builds a character through the use of key words and various ways of speaking. They will see that Helena's character is distinguishable from the other lovers'.

Starter (10 minutes)

The characters of Lysander and Demetrius are barely distinguishable: they are both passionate, though changeable, in love, and they are both aggressive in a fight. Suggest that Shakespeare does something quite different with the women.

Main phase (45 minutes)

Hermia and Helena are different from each other.

Ask the students quickly, in groups, to read all of Helena's lines up to this point in the play. One group should take on 1.1, a second 2.1, a third 2.2, a fourth 3.2.128–219, a fifth 3.2.220–434. They should pick out her metaphors and similes, such as 'your eyes are lodestars', and that comparison of Hermia's singing with a lark's; as well as all the horticultural references in the speech on line.

When they mention the lines beginning 'like two artificial gods' (3.2.203) draw out how the simile is extended to a point that is almost ridiculous: 'gods . . . needles . . . sampler . . . cushion . . . warbling . . . incorporate'.

Ask the students, in their groups, to look over the quarrel between Helena and Hermia (3.2, lines 191–377). If necessary, they might count the lines given to each character. What is striking? To use a modern phrase, Hermia can hardly get a word in edgeways. Suggest that Shakespeare is showing us that Helena *talks too much*.

Point out that Shakespeare gives Helena slightly cumbersome personifications – 'hasty-footed time' is one example – as well as long speeches and at least one convoluted metaphor.

On the other hand, Helena has one line that is the moral centre of the play: 'Love looks not with the eyes, but with the mind' (1.1.234). Ask the students to find it. Discuss: What exactly does it mean? And is it true?

Ask the students to write a modern version of this line.

Plenary (5 minutes)

Helena is concerned with the truth. She says at 3.2.129: 'When truth kills truth, O devilish-holy fray!' 'Devilish-holy' is an oxymoron. There are many oxymorons in *Romeo and Juliet*, and indeed throughout the early plays.

Helena: a character study

Act 3 Scene 2, lines 198–211

1. Helena and Hermia have been close friends for a long time. In groups, work out all the things that they have done together. 'Chid the hasty-footed time' means that they have told time off for going so quickly while they were enjoying being together.

   Write some lines about a close friend that you have known since, perhaps, nursery school. Pack the lines with activities you used to enjoy together. Your poem might be like Helena's lines from 'We, Hermia', just celebrating; or it might be a poem about someone you don't see now, or who is no longer a friend. Then it will have lines like Helena's regretful lines at the beginning of this extract.

2. In groups, collect some adjectives for Helena's character: 'well-read', 'bookish', 'humourless', 'decent' are some possibilities. Ask them to design a suitable costume and environment for her. In one production, she is short-sighted, and wears glasses.

   You might give her a pile of books to carry around, or set her in a private library. Exaggerate your idea of Helena for comic effect.

   Sometimes Helena appears an unattractive character. Find places where she seems self-pitying and where she seems to exaggerate her own unattractiveness.

3. Helena certainly has a lot to say! Some of the most difficult acting is done without words. In groups, one student should take the part of Helena in her speech beginning 'Lo, she is one of this confederacy!' (192). The other students should be Hermia, and listen with great care to what Helena says, and react to each line or group of lines. Indignance? Ignorance? Incomprehension? Anger?

4. Do a character study of one of the other lovers. Begin by reading all that character's lines individually, and then sharing what you have discovered. In twos write a short report on that person: a school report, perhaps, or notes by another character in a private diary. What would Lysander, for example, write about Demetrius?

5. Note 'devilish-holy' at line 129. Find oxymorons in *Romeo and Juliet*. Look, for example, at Act 1 Scene 1, lines 167ff and Act 3 Scene 2, lines 75ff.

6. 'Love looks not with the eyes, but with the mind' says Helena at 1.1.234. In groups discuss whether this is true to your experience.

7. 'Helena is over the top in all she says'. 'Helena is the only decent person in the play'. Go for one of these sentences, and defend it. Talk about it first, and then write down your views.

8. Imagine that you are directing the play. Using your sketch, write notes for the wardrobe master/mistress on how to dress Helena. Advise the actor: what hand gestures, movements, tricks of voice might be appropriate?

24

Lovers' insults

Various lines from Act 3 Scene 2: available online and at the end of this book.

Introduction

In this scene, Puck's mischief leads to the break-up of Hermia and Lysander, and powerful insults exchanged by her and Helena. Note that though only extracts from the scene are presented online, the students need to become familiar with all of it.

Aims

The students will appreciate the vigour of Shakespeare's language in a mode very different from much of the play. This scene differs greatly from Oberons's speech at 2.2.249ff ('I know a bank') and Titania's lines about climate disturbance in 2.1.87 ('But with thy brawls') to take two examples. They will distinguish between Helena and Hermia as characters.

Starter (10 minutes)

Using question and answer, recap the plot so far, especially as it concerns the lovers: in Act 1, Hermia and Lysander were in love, in defiance of Hermia's father, who wanted his daughter to marry Demetrius. Neither man had any time for Helena, who loved Demetrius. In Act 2, Helena followed Demetrius hopelessly into the wood. In 2.2, Puck put the juice into Lysander's eyes, and Lysander saw Helena first, and fell 'in love' with her. He deserted Hermia while she was asleep.

In this scene, Demetrius, in love with Hermia as he has been from the beginning, follows her. While he sleeps, Puck puts the potion in his eyes, and he sees Helena. So now Hermia, not Helena, is the despised woman . . .

Main phase (45 minutes)

First, point up the contrast in Shakespeare's writing in this play, using the examples given above compared with the robust insults in this scene.

Ask the students to study the insults as suggested on the task sheets. One teacher downplays or even ignores the lines where Lysander calls Hermia an 'Ethiop' and a 'tawny Tartar'. She also ignores the Third Witch's lines in *Macbeth* (Act 4 Scene 1) about the 'blaspheming Jew' and, once again, the Tartar. She feels that they are 'racist': an anachronism, as the earliest uses of the word are mid-twentieth century.

Ask: should a production of the play cut them or leave them in? Students should think about this for a moment, then share their views in groups. Each group has to come back to the rest of the class with a considered statement.

Tackling these lines head-on might usefully lead to discussion about bigotry. On the other hand, it might cause offence and seem to condone prejudice.

Lines 317–344: Ask the students to think of ways of presenting this. Would a scuffle between the two women be right? First they might present it as a radio play, with all the violence done with voices; then on an improvised stage: they must, first of all, take steps to be safe.

Some questions and issues that acting these lines present:
- What are the men doing as the women quarrel?
- What, for example, might Lysander be doing at line 321? Does his line suggest some action on his part?
- Should this scene be played for laughs or seriously? Again, raise this as an issue for discussion in groups.

Plenary (5 minutes)

Find out what the groups have decided about the 'racist' insults, and how the scene should be played.

Lovers' insults

Various lines from Act 3 Scene 2

1   Make a diagram or a pair of diagrams to fix the lovers' plot so far in their memories. They should show who loves whom at the end of each act.

2   Insults: Shakespeare certainly knew how to write effective ones! Examine all the insults the lovers use throughout the whole of this scene – not just the lines above – and divide them into groups. You might start with insults that involve comparisons with animals. Others are of a personal nature. Build up the list like this:

> **Animal insults**
> 'I had rather give his carcase to my hounds' – Demetrius to Hermia about Lysander, line 64.
> 'Out, cur! Out, dog!' – Hermia to Demetrius, line 64.

There are several other categories that you might come up with after group discussion.

3   The insults are loaded with prejudice: we can tell that Hermia is short, for example. Talk in groups about prejudice that you or friends of yours have experienced because of an aspect of their appearance.

4   Note that two of the insults are what we would today call 'racist'.

Can we call them racist in the context of the play? The word was unknown in Shakespeare's time. Or is that irrelevant? Would it have been better had they not been repeated online? Are you offended that they have?

Compare with *Macbeth* Act 4 Scene 1, lines 26 and 29.

5   A fight. Practice the lines from 'Away, you Ethiop' (266) to 'cheek by jowl' (338) in groups of four. Discuss how you will say the speeches. For example, there might be a crescendo for Hermia from 'O, when she is angry' (323), the lines rising to a scream; some speeches might be begun almost before the previous one has ended; and what are the men doing while the women quarrel: not just standing about, that's for sure . . .

Each group should make a presentation for the rest of the class.

6   'When truth kills truth, O devilish-holy fray!' says Helena. Another of the lovers mentions the importance of the truth near the end of the play. Who is it? Who does he or she make his comment to?

© Fred Sedgwick, 2011. *Resources for Teaching Shakespeare: 11–16.*

25

What vision . . .
a most rare vision

Act 4 Scene 1, lines 72–76 and 200–208: available online and at the end of this book.

Introduction

This is a turning point in the play. Two central characters wake up from strange dreams, and problems are solved.

Aims

The students will see parallels between Titania's experience and Bottom's; they will also learn more about Bottom's character. They will experience a soliloquy utterly unlike those in *Macbeth*; and they will see, once again, how change is critical to this play.

Starter (15 minutes)

Revise events so far, especially these: the mix-up with the lovers; the quarrel between the fairy king and queen; the preparations for the play to be put on in the forest.

Ask the students to re-read all Bottom's lines so far, and to discuss in groups what they already know about his character. In 1.2, according to one critic, his behaviour is like that of a child. He thinks he can do anything; he is unable to see the world except as it appears to him. Ask the students to read the speech that begins 'That will ask some tears . . .' in 1.2 as a child at some kind of pretend play.

Main phase (35 minutes)

Again in groups, ask the students to prepare a performance of Bottom's words that end this scene. They might change speakers at each punctuation mark, though the words from 'The eye of man' to 'what my dream was' should be spoken by the same speaker.

Or they might do it individually. It helps sometimes to walk a speech, changing direction as it feels right to do so.

Or they might find other ways of performing it.

Ask them to take turns to perform Titania's lines, with other students playing Oberon and Puck. Titania and Bottom have a word in common: 'Methought'. Indeed, Bottom says it three times in a short space of time. Suggest that this tells us something about these two characters: 'Me . . . me . . . me . . .'

Point out that this scene, taken as a whole, is unique in the play so far, because two of the three worlds – fairies and mechanicals – of the play are all present, and the court, Theseus and Hyppolita, are about to turn up.

Change again: Oberon has changed since the play began. Ask the students to compare his way of speaking in 4.1, especially lines 77–79, with his manner in 2.1. Ask: who else has changed (or has been changed)? Ask the students to make a list, with a note for each one, on the nature of the change.

Plenary (10 minutes)

When the students have acted Bottom's speech, offer them the following comments from the critic Harold Bloom:

'Bottom is as shrewd as he is kind . . . his response is always admirable . . . he is the favourite of his fellow mechanicals . . . there is no darkness in Bottom.'

Lead a discussion on these ideas. Note first what the other actors say about him at the beginning of 5.1.

What vision . . . a most rare vision

1 MAN BECOMES ASS AND BECOMES MAN AGAIN
   This is a terrible version of a headline. Think up a better one, and then write 'red top' versions of Bottom's adventure. Include interviews with Peter Quince and Bottom himself. Note that newspaper stories give the most surprising aspects first, and emphasise the sensational.

2 Talk in groups about times when you have woken from dreams. Scribble down, as quickly as you can, without thinking about it, what you remember from one dream. Try to capture your thinking as you recall things, in fits and starts, much as Bottom does.
   Write an account of a dream beginning with one of the following lines:

   'What visions have I seen!'
   'Methought I was'

3 Bottom is very alone when he says his words. His friends have run away, and the lovers have left just before he wakes. His speech is, in fact, a soliloquy. Practise saying his words, taking turns, making that aloneness evident. For example, if you have the space, one student might say them in the middle of a hall, or in a space on the field, with the rest of the students as the audience some metres from him. Take it in turns to sound alone. Turn frequently, as if looking for a friend to talk to.
   The actor has to do two things: make him or herself audible, and yet convince his audience that he is thinking.

3 Everyone went to church in Shakespeare's time. Bottom is nearly quoting a Bible passage everyone would have been familiar with. Find that passage, and compare it with Bottom's words: it is in the New Testament, in the first Epistle to the Corinthians, Chapter 2.

4 Do you agree with Oberon ('this hateful fool', line 46) and Puck ('fool', line 81) in their assessment of Bottom's character? He can be wise – see his answer to Titania in 3.1 when she says 'I love thee'. Go through the play, collecting evidence from his words and from other characters' words both to and about him that suggest that, first, he is wise; and, second, that he is a fool.

5 In many ways, Bottom is like a child. What childlike behaviour does he show early in the play?

6 In groups of three, act Titania's awakening. How does Oberon react? How does he say 'There lies your love'? How does Puck react?

7 'I was enamoured of an ass'. This is doting! Is 'doting' something sick, corrupt . . . ? Revise what you learnt about that word.

26

A local habitation and a name

Act 5 Scene 1, lines 4–17: available online and at the end of this book.

Introduction

Here are some of Shakespeare's most famous lines. Because of their music and their fame, they present a potential problem: bardolatry, that unthinking worship of Shakespeare.

Aims

The students will see and hear these lines without any of the heritage baggage: the 'sublime beauty' of Shakespeare's words. They will know that it is a mistake to talk of 'What Shakespeare says …' when it is one of his characters, not the playwright, himself who is speaking.

The students will examine Theseus' words and try to assess whether they are true to their own experience. And, more important, they will ask themselves what Theseus himself believes about lunatics, lovers and poets.

And they will explore the use of the word 'eye' (and associated words) throughout the play.

Starter (15 minutes)

The students need to know that, traditionally, dark faces were not considered 'fair' in either sense of the word in English culture of the period: hence 'brow of Egypt'. They have seen some of this in Chapter 24 and in their thinking about the lovers' insults.

Main phase (35 minutes)

Ask the students to illustrate the lines: 'The poet's eye, in a fine frenzy rolling, / Doth glance from heaven to earth, from earth to heaven …'

Ask them to write the lines in language suitable for a modern soap opera, replacing 'devils', 'hell', 'madman', 'lover', 'frantic', 'beauty' and others; the use of thesauruses is necessary. Ask them to share what they have written in groups.

'Sees', 'eye', 'glance' are important in this speech. Ask the students to scour the first three acts of the play for usages of 'eye', 'eyes' and 'eyne'. They might include associated words, such as 'sight', 'see', 'seest', etc. They should do this individually and then share their findings in groups, then sharing their results. Up to 2.2.14, there are some thirty-three examples.

They should make notes about each usage – who says the word, the context.

Sometimes, the word 'eyes' appears as 'eyne'. The students may suggest that Shakespeare has used this word to supply a rhyme in couplets. But: point out that 'eyne' as a plural had fallen out of use in the fourteenth century, and, like the use of rhyming couplets in plays, was old-fashioned.

Ask the students to write down modern sentimental sayings about love. They could collect some from Valentine cards to be seen in card shops in the high street, and write their own versions.

Plenary (10 minutes)

Ask one of the students to read Theseus' words again, in as inflated a way as possible. But other students should shout 'I never may believe / These antique fables …' wherever it seems appropriate.

A local habitation and a name

1. Illustrate the lines 'The poet's eye, in a fine frenzy rolling, / Doth glance from heaven to earth, from earth to heaven . . .' with a drawing, which could be used later as a sketch for a painting.

2. Find out about the beauty of Helen of Troy. Throughout literature, from ancient Greek times to the present, she has been a symbol of womanly beauty. Make notes about what you find.

3. Read the speech silently. Then, in groups, read it again, changing speakers at punctuation marks. Use a dictionary for any difficulties with meaning. Discuss what Theseus means.

4. Using a thesaurus, write a version of lines 9–13. The thesaurus will offer many options for, say, mad: 'unhinged', 'disturbed' and so on.

   Here is an example:

   > The insane person sees far more demons than can fit into the underworld. The betrothed is just as wild, seeing perfection in an ugly face. And then poet, as though in a fit, looks up and down, to heaven to earth, from earth to heaven . . .

5. Reflect on this part of Theseus' speech silently. Is it true, especially about the lover? Discuss this in groups. Think about anyone you know who is in love. Describe their behaviour. If you know a poet, does his eye 'roll in a frenzy'?

6. Go back to the first scene of the play. We can see there that the relationship between Theseus and Hyppolita, first, began in battle, and second, seems rather formal. Neither of them seems to be 'in a fine frenzy'. Now read Hyppolita's answer to Theseus' lines here. The first word tells you something important: 'But . . .' Write down some sentences with the title 'Theseus and his bride: a happy marriage . . . or not?' Quote from the play to back up your points.

7. You could do the same with Oberon and Titania.

8. Hyppolita says that, strange as the events of the night were, there was a 'constancy' about them. Look this word up and write down a sentence saying what Hyppolita means. Compare and contrast 'constancy' and 'frenzy'.

9. Find the word 'eyes' or any other associated words in the first two acts of the play. How many there are! Words to do with sight appear at least twelve times in the 86 lines between 56 and 242. Put each usage of any word to do with sight in the context of its line or even speech. For example, Helena uses 'eyes' in the same line as 'doting' (1.1.230).

10. Recall Helena's comment: 'Love looks not with the eyes but with the mind'. Discuss whether this is true.

27

An anthology of bad verse

Act 5 Scene 1, lines 71–3 and 118–125: available online and at the end of this book.

Introduction

There is a complete change of mood between the end of Theseus' speech in the last section and the rest of 5.1. From now on, the play moves amiably in a comic mode to the end.

Aims

The students will appreciate again the range of Shakespeare's writing – from the seductive if dubious sublimity of his writing of Theseus' meditations, to his writing of broad comedy.

They will have an opportunity to see how Shakespearean comedy can work in practice.

Starter (10 minutes)

Ask the students to read individually Theseus' lines earlier in the scene where he reads the list of plays on offer (lines 44–60). Then they should read them again, with a different voice for each play; and with a fifth voice for Theseus' rejection of each one.

Some explanations are needed to help them in their reading: for example, 'tipsy Bacchanals' were drunken women from Ovid's poem *Metamorphoses* who tore the singer Orpheus to pieces. They should know something about the muses: the Greeks believed there was one for each of the arts: Calliope for epic poetry, Clio for history, Erato for love poetry and so on.

Main phase (45 minutes)

Ask the students to study Quince's speech on line 71 onward. Ask them what seems to be wrong with it: Theseus knows. Quince ignores the points (punctuation marks).

Now ask the students to prepare two readings each of the speech. In one, they should say it as the punctuation demands. For the other, they should collaborate in writing the speech out with conventional punctuation, and then say it as this conventional punctuation demands.

Ask them to study Quince's long speech (lines 126–150). They should read it first individually, then in groups, and finally once more in groups, identifying all the bad poetry: the forced rhyme on the last syllable of 'certain', for example, the ludicrous way Quince gives the adjective 'vile' to an inanimate object, and the ridiculous overuse of alliteration near the end. Point the students in the direction of an earlier example of bad poetry, and ask them, once again, what is wrong with it (see Chapter 18, 'The raging rocks . . .'.

Plenary (5 minutes)

Collect and summarise all the students' findings about bad verse in the play. Why has Shakespeare written these lines like this?

An anthology of bad verse

Act 5 Scene 1, lines 71–3 and 118–125

1. Look at lines 44 to 60 where Theseus reads out the titles and summaries of the other plays on offer. In some productions, Philostrate reads the title of each play, and Theseus gives his reasons for rejecting it. Play the lines as if for a radio play in both ways: which seems the most effective?

2. More oxymorons: in lines 56–60, Theseus notes the oxymorons in the description of the play they are about to see, and adds some of his own. For more on oxymorons, look back at Helena's long speech in 3.2. There will be many more in *Romeo and Juliet*. Scour the play, and write down every oxymoron you find, and make a note about its context.

3. Look at Quince's lines from 108 onward. There is, of course, something seriously wrong with what he is saying. Write a description of today's weather with the punctuation all over the place. Read it to each other aiming for laughs.

    Now write both your weather report and Quince's speech out with 'proper' punctuation. Quince's speech might begin by leaving out the comma at the end of the first line.

4. Three students should be Theseus, Lysander and Hyppolita, and say their lines that come after Quince's lines. What tone will they adopt? Notice each of them has a simile for the way Quince speaks his lines: like 'a rough colt', 'a child on a recorder' and 'a tangled chain'. Are they competing with each other for 'best simile of the day?'

    Everyone else in the class should be Quince. How does he react to their comments? Incomprehension? Annoyance? Irritability?

5. Quince will no doubt tell his wife later about how it all went. Write a speech for him, either in Shakespearean language, or in language to suit a modern soap opera.

6. Now the play moves cheerfully in a comic mode to the end. But there are darker moments. For example, neither Theseus nor Hyppolita are laughing at the actors, however bad their play is, and however badly they have acted, at lines 272–273. Discuss: what might be going through their minds at this point?

7. In groups, find each of the longer speeches from the play within the play: Quince (twice, 'If we offend . . .' and 'Gentles, perchance . . .'); Snout ('In this same interlude . . .'); Bottom (twice again, 'O grim-looked night! . . .' and 'Sweet moon . . .') and Snug ('You ladies . . .'). Take turns to read them as funnily as possible. Then choose one speech, memorise it, and perform it to another class, or the whole school.

28

Thou lob of spirits . . .

Act 5 Scene 1, lines 349–368: available online and at the end of this book.

Introduction

The problem of the fairy stereotype has to be addressed: many students will (rightly) be put off by the image of the transparently winged mini-humans hovering at the end of the garden.

Aims

The students will understand something of Puck's character, and they will reflect on different ways in which an actor and producer might break the fairy stereotype.

Starter (10 minutes)

In Shakespeare's day fairies were seen as human-sized and often full of bad intent towards humans. Emphasise that Puck is part of the fairy world of this play, a kind of sidekick to the king Oberon, a character with power.

Ask the students to note what the fairy at the beginning of 2.1 calls Puck: 'lob' and 'Robin Goodfellow'. These are terms for a creature of English folklore – a loutish, hairy man who did household jobs in return for a saucer of milk. Edward Thomas's poem 'Lob' describes him with his various names:

> Jack Smith, Jack Moon, poor Jack of every trade,
> Young Jack, or old Jack, or Jack What-d'ye-call,
> Jack-in-the-hedge, or Robin-run-by-the-wall,
> Robin Hood, Ragged Robin, lazy Bob,
> One of the lords of No Man's Land . . .

Main phase (45 minutes)

Ask the students to arrange themselves in groups, and to divide the play up between each member. Leaving out Act 1, in which Puck doesn't appear, ask them to read all of Puck's lines.

Then they should discuss what Puck's functions are in the play. For example, he moves the plot along; he acts as a chorus, telling us what has happened; he is a foil for Oberon. It is helpful to think of the play without him – almost as strange a thought as *Hamlet* without the Prince.

Ask the students to take one speech from each act, and then to prepare a performance of it. For example, 'I am that merry wanderer of the night' (2.1.44ff) might be performed with other students miming 'lurking in a gossip's bowl', and the other actions. 'Through the forest I have gone (2.2.72ff), with its short lines, needs the nervy, jerky movements of someone hunting through the undergrowth with a stick; 'On the ground' (3.2.448ff) requires a more gentle, compassionate reading; and the one given online here requires much slower movements.

Plenary (5 minutes)

Suggest that the students think differently about fairies, and give them this quotation: Peter Hall, the producer of a groundbreaking production of *A Midsummer Night's Dream* at Stratford in 1969, spoke witheringly of 'fairies in little white tutus, skipping through gossamer forests'.

Thou lob of spirits . . .

1   Design a costume for Puck. Be imaginative and daring – the only rule is nothing fairy-like!

   Find the scene where the other fairies – Mustardseed, Peaseblossom, Cobweb, Moth and his friends – attend upon Bottom. Design costumes for them that match Puck's, but also contain some element of each character's name.

2   In groups of eight, divide into pairs, with each pair working on one act out of Acts 2, 3, 4 and 5. Each pair should scour their act, reading every one of Puck's lines. Decide which speech most encapsulates Puck's character. The groups should then share their findings. Defend your choices, saying why you have made them.

   If you can, take this further. Which *word* in your chosen line says most about Puck?

3   Imagine a production of the play where you are either the actor playing Puck, or the director. Make notes:

   - How old will your Puck be? He has often been played as a naughty boy, but in one film production, he was bald, middle-aged and rather fed up.
   - Bear in mind that in Shakespeare's time, there were no female actors. We can be much more flexible today – what would a female Puck be like?
   - How will he move? There are hints about this in some of his lines. In some productions he appears to fly. Take a hint from the point in Act 2 where we find out how long it takes him to fly round the earth.
   - What is his relationship with Oberon like? Write a note written by Oberon called 'My servant Puck'.

4   Pick any two speeches in the play longer than ten lines, one by Puck, and the other by Bottom.

   Make two columns on a sheet of paper, one headed 'Bottom', the other 'Puck'. Write words under each name that say something about the character's personality.

   What other comments would you make about Puck, when you compare him to Bottom?

5   The play began with two mentions of the moon in the first four lines. Now, as it ends, Puck mentions the moon again. Look through the play and find as many mentions of the moon (and moonshine) that you can, and makes notes on them. Build on what you have already learnt in Section 2. Write:

   - a short essay called 'The Moon in *A Midsummer Night's Dream*'
     or
   - a poem called 'Moonlight'.

Write a mini-saga of the story of the play. It should have no more than fifty words – and, if possible, exactly that. You will find that, by trying to keep to a strict limit, you will discover what to you are the most important elements in the play, and what is less important.

Section 3   *Romeo and Juliet*

In fair Verona . . .

Prologue and Act 1 Scene 1, lines 5–26: available online and at the end of this book.

Introduction

In some ways, Act 1 Scene 1 is the perfect scene to introduce Shakespeare to young people. It has none of the grand, impenetrable language some students expect. It is downright earthy.

Aims

The students will note the difference in tone between the Prologue's words and those spoken in 1.1. There will be more about this later in section 7, but it worth alerting students now to the fact that contrasts between consecutive scenes present just one of the oppositions in the play. Second, students will see that Shakespeare is a writer concerned with ordinary human beings, with some of the same obsessions as they have.

Starter (5 minutes)

Read the Prologue in the tone of one of the following:
* the Chorus on the Tudor stage
* a history teacher introducing a new subject
* a headteacher beginning a story in assembly in which he/she doesn't feel involved
* a newsreader on television.

Emphasise the tortuous grammar, especially in lines 7–9, and also the way the Chorus gives away the ending of the story.

Main phase 45 minutes

Ask the students to read 1.1, lines 5–26. Point out, first, that there is a contrast between the Prologue's lines and these. Ask the student: what makes this contrast? They should share their thoughts in groups. The most obvious change is that the lines in the Prologue are in verse, and the lines in the second are in prose. Two changes are related to this: the Chorus's words are formal while Sampson and Gregory's words are streetwise and vulgar. And the Prologue has over a dozen adjectives in merely fourteen lines while the servants speak largely in nouns and verbs.

Ask three students to read the lines from the beginning of 1.1 up to Benvolio's first words, 'Part, fools!' They should do this first in a place out of the classroom; next they rehearse the lines, still away from the rest of the class; and then they should make a presentation to everybody. Some of the students may laugh, with varying degrees of embarrassment at certain points. (It might be a worry if they don't.) Some examples are:
* 'thrust his maids to the wall'; 'maidenheads'; 'pretty piece of flesh'; 'naked weapon'.

Any such laughter should be encouraged: the gigglers are already getting at the heart of a large part of this play. Its repetitive sexual innuendo is a counterpoint to the play's central theme of true love. Some examples of sexual innuendo in this scene are:
* 'valiant to stand'
* 'take the wall of any man or maid' (the wall joke is extended in subsequent lines)
* the 'heads' / 'maidenheads' joke
* 'feel it'
* 'pretty piece of flesh'.

Now ask the whole class, in threes, to prepare presentations of these lines.

Plenary 10 minutes

Explain the abab manner of recording rhyme, so that the students can analyse the rhyme of the first scene (which is, of course, a sonnet: the rhyme scheme is abab cdcd efef gg).

In fair Verona . . .

1　Think: what subjects do you discuss with your friends – television, music, other friends? Write a dialogue between two modern young people, spoken as they drift around the streets of your town, your village.

2　Look at the Prologue. (The word comes from the Greek *pro* 'before' and *logos* 'speech'.) How many ways can you think of performing it? Think about this individually, and then share your ideas in groups.

　　Practise saying it.

　　It might be done very fast, breathlessly – we can't wait to get on with the story – but every word must be audible.

　　It might be done with an air that something very important is about to be shown.

3　Count the lines in the prologue, and record the rhyme scheme like this: lines 1 and 3 rhyme, so call them both a; lines 2 and 4 rhyme, so call them both b and so on, using a new letter every time there is a new rhyme.

4　Individually, pick out the crucial words in the Chorus' speech – words which might well suggest the themes and moods of the play. Share your words with your neighbour, and then in groups. Argue for your words! Notice how some words are emphasised by repetition of their sounds: 'forth' / 'fatal'; 'Doth' / 'death' / 'strife' / 'death'.

5　Count the syllables in each line: there are ten. Find out what this kind of poem is called. Shakespeare wrote over 150 of them outside the plays: the most famous begins, 'Shall I compare thee to a summer's day?' Find it. Learn some or all of it by heart.

6　Act 1 Scene 2 takes place on an Italian street. The characters are ordinary people, the servants of the Montagues. Read Gregory's lines, then Sampson's. What do you discover about their characters? (first, ways in which they are similar, and, second, ways in which they differ).

　　Which of the two is the most boastful? The braver?

7　Identify instances of sexual innuendo in lines 1–28.

8　'Double entendre'. You may well know that this is a French phrase that means, literally, 'double hearing'. This scene is packed with double entendres: most of the sexual jokes fit this description, but others are puns without sexual connotations. There are two very sombre double entendres later – one as Mercutio dies, and one spoken by the Captain at the end of the play. Can you find them?

9　Someone has said about these lines, 'I don't know why Shakespeare begins this particular play like this. It would be better if it began at line 56 when Tybalt arrives . . . we don't need the servants and their smut!'

　　What do you think? Write a note called either 'The opening 55 lines of *Romeo and Juliet* – dump them' or 'Why the opening 55 lines of *Romeo and Juliet* are important'.

10　You have been asked to produce the play. Here, there is a brawl between the Montagues and the Capulets. How will you help the audience to distinguish between them? In one production, the families wore different football colours!

　　Or would you bother?

30

O brawling love . . .
fiend angelical!

Act 1 Scene 1, lines 166–173 and Act 3 Scene 2, lines 73–79: available online and at the end of this book.

Introduction

Oxymoron and paradox are central to Shakespeare's language in his early plays (and elsewhere, especially in *Macbeth*: 'Fair is foul', and so on).

Aims

The students will first understand what these words mean, and second, begin to appreciate their power in Shakespeare's hands. Later they will add 'oppositions' to this list (see Chapter 35 on the Friar).

Starter (5 minutes)

Write up:

OXYMORON

Tell the students that the word is formed from the Greek *oxys* ('sharp') and *moros* ('stupid'). They will probably infer what it means from this etymology.

Similarly,

PARADOX

is from the Greek *para* ('contrary') and *doxa* ('opinion').

Usually, oxymorons are formed by words, one of which follows immediately after the other, while paradoxes are formed by words that are separated.

Main phase (45 minutes)

Point out that the two speeches given online are almost entirely composed of oxymorons and paradoxes. Ask them in pairs to prepare a reading of Romeo's lines from Act 1 where each student speaks a word in an appropriate way. For example, 'brawling' should be spoken in the voice of a ruffian, and 'love' in the voice of, say, a boy/girlfriend. They should accompany the words with actions.

Ask the students to do the same with Juliet's lines from Act 2.

Then put Juliet's raging oxymorons in context: her Nurse has told her that Romeo, her lover, has killed her kinsman, Tybalt. Ask the students to examine 3.2 from the entry of the Nurse (line 31) to 'O serpent heart' (line 73). They should ask themselves questions, and find provisional answers, jotting them down straightaway:

- What are the Nurse's feelings? How will she express them with her movements? What is in her mind when she says the line beginning 'Alack the day . . .'?

Now in twos they should prepare readings of the scene.

Juliet's feelings have a long journey to travel between the Nurse's entry and her finally stating the truth in line 70. The student playing her must start with apprehension at 'what news'; move to horror when she thinks that Romeo is dead; then – to whatever terrible feelings she will have when she hears that Romeo is alive, but that he is the banished killer of her cousin. The pairs should work on this for some time.

Plenary (10 minutes)

If there is more time, some of the pairs should produce their performance (lines 35–70).

O brawling love . . . fiend angelical!

Act 1 Scene 1, lines 166–173 and Act 3 Scene 2, lines 73–79

Oxymorons

These speeches are together online because they are full of oxymorons and paradoxes. Familiarity with these ideas will help you in your study not only of *Romeo and Juliet* but also of *A Midsummer Night's Dream*. If you have already studied *Macbeth*, you might have concluded already that it is one huge paradox: 'Fair is foul and foul is fair . . .'

1 Find oxymorons elsewhere in this play. One possibility near the beginning of the play sums up the plot. And another, near the end of 2.2, has become something people say when parting from a friend.

2 Make a list of your own oxymorons. The two conflicting, contradicting, opposite words should appear together: examples are 'low height' and 'mad wisdom'.

3 Then make a list of your own paradoxes. The words are separated. An example is 'You have come far in wisdom, but it has made you stupid'. Look now at Friar Lawrence's speech at the beginning of Act 2 Scene 3, and make a note of his several oppositions.

4 Practise ways of acting, first for a radio play, and then for the stage, these two speeches of Romeo and Juliet. For the stage, ask questions of each other: How does Romeo move as he says these lines? Where does Juliet look as she says hers? Is she still, sitting on her bed? Does she move around the set? Both actors have to express frustration.

5 The sound 'I' in 3.2, lines 45–52: Shakespeare loves puns and wordplay. We mostly think of puns as light-hearted word games – see the pun in the first four lines of the play, which you can sum up like this: 'coals' . . . 'colliers' (coal-miners) . . . 'choler' (temper) . . . 'collar'. Later, watch out for Mercutio's puns.

   Now look at lines spoken by the Nurse and Juliet, immediately after the Nurse has told Juliet about Tybalt's death (3.2.45–52). Their situation couldn't be worse – but the puns come thick and fast. Working as individuals, find the most common vowel sound in these lines. Write down every appearance of that sound. Share your findings with a partner. Note that 'ay' was pronounced like our 'eye'. Read the lines again, emphasising that sound. Note that two words that are not part of the pun sequence also emphasise the main vowel sound.

6 Look at Romeo's lines in 1.1. Who is he in love with here? He doesn't name the girl: find out who it is by reading carefully all his conversations with Benvolio in this scene and in 1.2. Then find the moment at the Capulets' party when he stops being in love with that person.

7 Sir John Suckling (1609–1642) wrote:

> Out upon it, I have loved
>   Three whole days together;
> And am like to love three more,
>   If it prove fair weather . . .

Romeo's first love doesn't last long. Write a poem that begins: 'Lovers will love so short a time . . .'

31

A fair assembly

Act 1 Scene 2, lines 34–43 and 63–72: available online and at the end of this book.

Introduction

This is a minor passage. But Shakespeare's 'lowlife', here represented by the Servant, matter. This man is a minor forerunner of Sir John Falstaff in the history plays, Feste in *Twelfth Night*, Touchstone in *As You Like It* and the Porter in *Macbeth*.

Aims

Students will see prose and verse working in the same scene, and some of the effect of the change; they will see how Shakespeare supplies comic relief with his clowns.

Starter (5 minutes)

Ask the students to look at the shape of Capulet's and Romeo's speeches compared to the shape of the Servant's. The upper classes speak in verse, the lower in prose. If they have studied *Macbeth* and *A Midsummer Night's Dream*, they might recall instances of this.

Capulet speaks verse even when he is saying the most ordinary things (lines 34–37). Why is this? He even rhymes. Possible answers:

- Upper class/tragedy is always verse.
- Lower class/comedy is always prose.

This over-simplification holds some truth.

Main phase (45 minutes)

Ask the students to study the Servant's speech. Then they should, individually, practise ways of saying it as for a radio play. The first sentence expresses the minor exasperation the Servant feels for his boss, which he dare not express to his boss's face. We all know this feeling. 'Bring that work to me by tomorrow morning'. We wait till we are alone, then: 'Tomorrow morning!'

They should think of adding action. To whom should the Servant address his lines? Himself? The heavens? The audience? An imaginary companion? Ask the students to prepare ways of acting the speech to the greatest comic effect, and then to try it out on each other. Comedians say that getting a laugh is all in the timing. A long pause at the first '!' perhaps? A long silent stare in each direction? And the last sentence: we all know that feeling, too: 'I must do that homework . . . In good time!'

There is much opportunity during Romeo's speech for comic business. When the students look at the complete script, they should work out what is happening between lines 44 and 62, just before Romeo reads the letter. They might assume that the Servant doesn't stand stock still – a very boring option – and that he is trying wordlessly to get Romeo's attention. Peering into Romeo's face? Tapping him on the shoulder?

Point out that, when Romeo starts to read Capulet's letter, he is simply doing the Servant a favour. There are potentially dramatic changes, though, at the mentions of two names. Make sure that the students appreciate the significance of 'Capulet' and 'Rosaline'.

Plenary (10 minutes)

Revise the prose/verse issue by reading aloud some of Capulet's lines, and some of the Servant's, making clear which is verse and which is prose.

A fair assembly

Act 1 Scene 2, lines 34–43 and 63–72

1 Look up 'last' in the dictionary. What does the word mean as a noun? What does 'yard' mean here?

2 The Servant has got everything wrong. There are two possible reasons for this: either he is dim, or he is pretending to be. Read his lines in silence four or five times, and make up your mind about the right reason. Then share your thinking in groups.

   Now perform the speech, first as though he is genuinely dim, and second as though he is merely pretending to be.

3 Imagine you are helping to produce a modern-dress production of the play. Make detailed drawings of the servant, first as a complete dimwit (ill-fitting, ill-matching clothes? Bad haircut? – be creative!) and second as a craftier character only pretending to be dim.

4 Update his speech: help him to express the same muddle, but with modern trades. Start with: 'It's said that the computer nerd should work on his sermons, that the priest should never get his cutting and pasting wrong . . .'

5 Benvolio and Romeo enter in the middle of a very serious conversation. Invent some comic business for the Servant: he wants a favour from them. Perhaps he wanders about clearing his throat, getting closer and closer. It looks from the script as though he interrupts Romeo in line 55. In threes (though Benvolio is silent), act the lines from this point to line 81. Make a contrast between the Servant and the two young men: their facial expressions, their manner of speaking – everything will be different.

6 One of Shakespeare's tragedies, *Richard II*, has no comic relief from clowns – characters like this servant. Make a case for saying that *Romeo and Juliet* would be a better play without all the servants, except for those that simply help to move the action along. Find the scenes where Gregory, Sampson, this Servant and the Nurse appear. Write a note entitled either:
   • 'Dump the clowns – making *Romeo and Juliet* a proper tragedy.'
       or
   • 'Thank goodness for the clowns in *Romeo and Juliet*.'

7 Romeo reads the letter that Juliet's father is sending round town. There are so many different tones of voice he might use. Think of some adjectives:
   • Sarcastic, mocking, uninterested, curious, willing simply to help the servant do his job.
   • At what point(s) does his tone and demeanour change?

8 The Servant doesn't do exactly what his master has told him to do. Check Capulet's orders and discuss why this might be.

32

A pretty age

Act 1 Scene 3, lines 11–25 and Act 2 Scene 5, selected lines: available online and at the end of this book.

Introduction and aims

These scenes are together because, first, they tell us much about the character of the Nurse, and about her relationships with Juliet and her mother. And, second, they also raise the issue of Juliet's age, and all that it implies.

Starter (10 minutes)

Revise the contexts for the two scenes. The first one takes place just after Romeo finds out about the Capulets' ball; by the time the events in the second take place, Paris is on the scene; Romeo and Juliet have fallen in love and have met in the window scene; Romeo has enlisted the Friar's help; and Romeo has given the Nurse a rope ladder so that he can get into her house.

Main phase (45 minutes)

Ask the students to read the Nurse's speech about Juliet's age. It will be Lammas-tide soon . . . Juliet was born on Lammas-Eve fourteen years ago. Present two points of view to be discussed in groups. First, Juliet is a child; under-age sex is always wrong and must be taken seriously in all contexts. Second, different times, different standards; or, when in Rome . . . or rather when in Verona do as the Veronese do . . . Shakespeare is not concerned with this issue, which has much more serious implications now than it had in his day: he is simply writing a love story.

Add to the discussion a suggestion that the students should imagine an episode in a soap opera where a character is about to get married before her fourteenth birthday.

You might also point out that the word 'paedophilia', though of Greek origin, is a recent coinage.

Ask the students to discuss these matters in groups. Each group should try to come up with an agreed position.

The Nurse. Ask the students to prepare in groups a reading of the Nurse's lines from 17 to 49, when Lady Capulet interrupts. They should change speakers often, at least at every punctuation mark, and sometimes more often. Point out that in some editions of the play, this speech is given as prose. How quickly can they say the speech without losing clarity?

Ask them to do the same on the long speech in 2.5. This time, one student should be Juliet, while others are the Nurse, taking turns to read her speech, again changing speakers at each punctuation mark.

Ask them to make notes about the character of the Nurse. They might refer to her talkativeness, her sentimentality, her absent-mindedness, her teasing, her dirty-mindedness.

Plenary (5 minutes)

Speak 1.3, lines 18–26 yourself, emphasising the speed, the absent-minded pauses, the changes of direction – and then change your manner suddenly at the mention of her dead daughter Susan – and speak the lines about her in a contrasting way: reflectively, even prayerfully.

Point out that Shakespeare's characters are never made of cardboard: even the silly ones have three dimensions.

Glossary

Teen: sorrow.

When Juliet uses the word 'news' she means it as a plural noun. Hence 'tell them'.

A pretty age

Act 1 Scene 3, lines 11–25 and Act 2 Scene 5, selected lines

The Nurse's speeches

1 After your reading of the whole of the Nurse's speech in Act 1 Scene 3, list individually and then in groups some adjectives and nouns that describe the Nurse's character: talkative is a start, but there should be many more.

2 Practise acting this long speech as an unstoppable torrent in groups of three. What might Lady Capulet and Juliet be doing all this time? It would be boring if they were just standing about on stage. What might a mother and daughter do with each other when they know that they have no chance of getting a word in? Female students may have contributions to make here. In one production, Lady Capulet spent much of the Nurse's speech half paying attention to the Nurse, and half preparing Juliet's hair for the dance. In another production, they wandered in and out of the room, paying no attention at all.

3 Bearing in mind that Lady Capulet is a mother, work out ways she might react to the lines about:
   * the Nurse's daughter Susan's death
   * the Nurse's late husband's sexual remarks about Juliet falling backward
   * the bump as 'big as a cock'rel's stone' on Juliet's brow
   * Juliet being 'the prettiest babe'.

All these reactions will tell us something about Lady Capulet's character. For example, is she merely impatient of the Nurse? Or does she remember her (and her husband and Susan) with affection? How does she react to memories of Juliet's childhood? Make notes on all these questions, and share them.

4 We are not sure whether the Nurse's speech in 1.3 was originally in prose or verse. Study it carefully, and write it out in prose. Decide individually whether a prose or a verse rendition suits it best.

5 Susan

Even characters we might laugh at have moments when we feel sympathy for them. Practise reading the lines about Susan in a different tone of voice from the one you might use for the rest of the speech.

   Write a short poem about what the Nurse felt just after the death of her baby, or about how she remembers her daughter whenever she sees Juliet: remember Susan and Juliet were 'of an age'.

6 We know Juliet's age exactly. Imagine that you have been asked to produce the play at school in modern dress, and to be as up-to-date as possible. The headteacher hears at rehearsal the Nurse's lines about Juliet's age, and objects. What will you do?
   * Agree with the headteacher: underage sex is always wrong. Cut the Nurse's lines.
   * Ask the actress to say these lines even faster than she does the other ones, in the hope that nobody notices
   * Point out certain lines: 1.3.67, 1.3.99–100 and 2.5.31–42, and say that Juliet is wiser than her years might suggest: the lines stay in.

As you go through the play, watch out for signs of Juliet's maturity.

33

Mercutio: a grave man

Act 2 Scene 1, lines 17–29 (Mercutio's lines only) and Act 3 Scene 1, lines 82–83, 89–90, 97–99: available online and at the end of this book.

Introduction
Mercutio is crucial to this play, and it is important that students pay close attention to his words.

Aims
The students will see how Shakespeare contributes to his building of a character in relatively few lines: the humour and gallantry of Mercutio.

Starter (10 minutes)
Ask the students if they can see any sexual jokes in the first extract (A). Discuss in groups, where they should compare them with the jokes in the early lines of the play.

Main phase (45 minutes)
There are jokes about estates ('demesnes' – but here sexual parts), semen, the vagina, erections and male sexual failure ('conjured it down'). How much of this is to be made explicit depends on the ethos of individual schools, and on the nature of the relationship each teacher has with his or her class. It is better that the sexual part of the double meanings should emerge in group discussion where possible:

Ask the students to work in groups. They should prepare a performance of Mercutio's lines (**A**) in which they share the words, swapping speakers at each punctuation mark or line ending. Critically, they must present the lines as though they are free of any sexual innuendo. Each group should present its version of the lines, done in this way.

At each presentation, the rest of the class is sternly instructed not to laugh.

Of course, this is impossible. Now ask the groups to identify the jokes, and what it was that made them laugh.

The more important question arises: Why, in this play of all plays, a play about what is considered traditionally a pure thing, the love of a young couple, does Shakespeare make Mercutio talk like this? (And why all that sexual wordplay in 1.1, and the Nurse's bawdy?)

Ask the groups to discuss this. You might suggest that Mercutio doesn't believe in true love, and reduces it all to sex, and that his views are a necessary counterpoint to the intense love of Romeo and Juliet. If he weren't in the play, that love might come across as sentimental.

Sometimes Mercutio is played as though he has an unrequited love for Romeo.

B

Ask the students to read the whole of the fight scene in groups. Ask some questions: Why does Shakespeare kill Mercutio? We are not yet halfway through the play.

Ask the students to find the longest speech in the play up to the point where he dies. Ask them to talk about this in groups: what is there in this speech that carries the action forward? Suggest that if Shakespeare hadn't killed him, Mercutio would have stolen the play from Romeo; and that, though he is full of poetry, Mercutio is a scene-stealer. Once he starts, he doesn't stop: he has to be stopped. So Shakespeare stopped him.

Plenary (5 minutes)
The 'Queen Mab' speech is glorious poetry. Go through it as a class, picking out the most striking lines. Suggest that they learn some of the speech by heart.

Mercutio: a grave man

Act 2 Scene 1, lines 17–29 (Mercutio's lines only) and Act 3 Scene 1, lines 82–83, 89–90, 97–99

1. Mercutio is a very different kind of character from any other in this play. Read his long speech in 1.1 beginning 'O then I see Queen Mab hath been with you'. Read it in groups, changing speakers at every punctuation mark or line ending – wherever it feels right to do so.

2. It's good to run wild sometimes. Write your own Queen Mab speech. One student wrote hers, and it began:

> O then I see Queen Mab hath been with you:
> She is the tree's bark shaper, and she comes
> In a shape as round as our earth itself,
> A small particle of magical fate,
> Travelling, floating with the natural breeze.
> Through polar bears' hairs she explores the ice.
> Her spherical carriage gracefully soars . . .

   This student has, first, kept her lines much the same length as Shakespeare's, and, second, she has done what Mercutio has done: she has let her imagination run wild. You should try to be as wild, imaginatively, as Mercutio.

3. Think in groups of adjectives to describe Mercutio based on the Queen Mab speech and the speech containing the lines 'I conjure thee'. You might begin with words meaning roughly these things: fantastical, exaggerated, filthy-minded. A thesaurus will be helpful.

4. Prepare a costume for Mercutio on his way to a fancy dress ball. First, sketch it, and then write a description of the cut and colours of the garments. Be sure his costume will be fancier than everyone else's.

5. Read the lines from 'I conjure thee' ('thee' is the moody Romeo) in different ways – as someone at a séance, for example, trying to raise a spirit from the other world.

6. Prepare a performance of 3.1, from line 66 (where Mercutio denounces Romeo's refusal to fight) to the exit of Mercutio and Benvolio at line 99. You will need to work in groups of three.

   Some suggestions:
   - Normally Mercutio speaks at length. Not here. The punctuation and the briefness of his utterances tell you how to perform this part. Notice the famous line 'A plague on both your houses!' How does each speaking of it differ? Notice that the last time he says it (or anything) it is much shortened.
   - Notice, too, how he still has time for grim jokes (the well and the church door) and a pun. How will the student playing him say these lines?
   - The first time you act these lines, act them as a radio play. Swap roles, and act the scene again with some action. Repeat a third time in whichever way seems the most effective.

7. You wrote down some words to describe Mercutio as he appeared earlier in the play. Now do the same for him as he appears in the scene where he is fatally stabbed.

8. Find a prose speech by Mercutio in 2.4 in which he names famous women in history. Their lives all have something in common. Find out what it is.

34

And palm to palm
is holy palmer's kiss

Act 1 Scene 5, lines 93–105 and Act 2 Scene 2, lines 25–55: available online and at the end of this book.

Introduction

This scene – Act 2 Scene 2 – is possibly the most common theatrical cliché of all, and it has been sent up by comedians and advertisers galore. The latest I have seen is a French advertisement for a comic novel. Juliet is a fat cat on her balcony, and Romeo is an innocent climbing mouse bearing flowers. 'How well you climb!' says the hungry predator.

Note that in Shakespeare there is no balcony!

Aims

Students will understand one of Shakespeare's most famous scenes – in fresh ways, derived from their own thinking about the script, not merely from convention; and they will see how Romeo especially uses religious imagery.

Starter (5 minutes)

The cliché effect is made worse by the fact that Juliet's line 'Romeo, Romeo, wherefore art thou Romeo?' is misunderstood by nearly everyone who hears it outside the context of the play. Ask the students what they think it means . . . and then point out that 'wherefore' means 'why', not 'where': Juliet wishes her lover was from a different family. She is not (that cliché again) gazing over the garden looking for him.

Main phase (50 minutes)

Ask the students, in groups, to take turns speaking Romeo's lines in the second extract (B). The others should call out at each point where he uses a word that has some religious significance.

Now ask them to refer back to 1.5, which is passage A online. Romeo has just seen Juliet for the first time. Two of the students should speak lines 92–109, and, once again, the other students should call out at each religious reference: 'profane . . . holy shrine . . . sin . . . pilgrim . . . palmer . . . saints . . . pray . . . faith . . . despair . . .' Juliet immediately picks up 'pilgrim' and changes it to 'palmer'. Point out that pilgrims came back from the Holy Land carrying palms, hence this name.

In groups, the students should work through all of Romeo's speeches up to the balcony scene, looking for his references to religion. There are at least two:

- At 1.2.88 he continues an argument with Benvolio by saying, 'When the devout religion of mine eye / Maintains such falsehood . . .'.
- At 1.4.112 he prays in the company of Mercutio and Benvolio: 'He that hath the steerage of my course / Direct my sail'.

Point out that the lines from 'If I profane with my unworthiest hand' to 'then love not while my prayer's effect I take' comprise a sonnet. They have already come across one sonnet in the play: direct them again to the Prologue. The effect of this sonnet, with its perfect rhyme and metre, suggests that the lovers are already profoundly in tune with each other.

Plenary (5 minutes)

Discuss with the whole class occasions when lovers have been separated by the difference of their origins. Talk with them about times when it happens today. The film *West Side Story* would be more than useful.

And palm to palm is holy palmer's kiss

Act 1 Scene 5, lines 93–105 and Act 2 Scene 2, lines 25–55

1 'Young men's love then lies / Not truly in their hearts, but in their eyes'. Find out who says this in the play. Discuss: is it true?

2 Romeo is definitely in love this time! Shakespeare makes that certain with the imagery he gives him.

    Lines 26–32 in 2.2 will become clearer if you make a drawing of that 'winged messenger of heaven . . . bestrid[ing] the lazy puffing clouds, / And sail[ing] upon the bosom of the air'.

    Then add to the drawing the 'white-upturned wond'ring eyes / Of mortals'.

    Your drawing will, if you do it well, become quite ridiculous. Don't worry about scale: 'the wond'ring eyes' could be huge, for example.

    Write Romeo's words on the drawing, and learn them by heart. Then note that the 'messenger of heaven' is what Juliet is like; compared to her, Romeo is, according to himself, a mortal.

    If you have time and resources, find out more about surrealist art, and make a surrealist painting based on these lines and your sketch.

3 Love is . . .
Near the beginning of the play, Romeo (still in love with Rosaline) said to his friend Benvolio 'Love is a smoke made from the fume of sighs, / Being purged, a fire sparkling in lovers' eyes, / Being vexed, a sea nourished with loving tears'.

    Write your own poem beginning 'Love is . . .' Your poem could be a kenning: a list of names you might give love. For example, here is the beginning of a kenning about hate: 'You are / an enraged dog / a fog that lasts / for days, weeks, months / years, years . . .'

4 Religious imagery
Romeo often uses Christian imagery. Find all his religious references throughout the play. Imagine that you have been asked to design a set for the play. How might you make use of religion? If you manage to see the Baz Luhrmann film, you will see a powerful use of Christian (specifically Catholic) imagery.

5 Read the conversations between Romeo and Benvolio in 1.1, 1.2 and 1.4. At one point, Romeo says: 'I am not for this ambling; / . . . I will bear the light'. He has nothing to talk about but love, love, love . . . Be Benvolio. Write to another friend, whether by note, email, text (this is in a very up-to-date production!). Start with:

    Saw Romeo today. He was so . . . it was like . . . I thought I would . . .

6 The predicament that Romeo and Juliet find themselves in has been common throughout history, and is not uncommon now. Human beings find enemies in terms of family background (as here), in terms of social class, in terms of race, in terms of religion.

    Discuss in groups, and write notes about times, whether fictional or factual, where lovers or just friends have been separated in such ways.

35

Good morrow, father

Act 2 Scene 3, lines 1–12: available online and at the end of this book.

Introduction
Friar Lawrence is an important character, first, because of his function in moving the plot along, and, second, because of his relationship to Romeo. Also, this speech echoes a constant theme in the play: oppositions.

Aims
The students will begin to understand the Friar and his dramatic purpose, and they will consolidate their learning about opposites/oxymorons/paradoxes.

Starter (10 minutes)
Ask the students to revise the work done on oxymorons: those spoken by Romeo in 1.1 and those by Juliet in 3.3: 'loving hate … fiend angelical …', and so on. They should say the two speeches again, emphasising the contradiction within each line or phrase.

Main phase (40 minutes)
Widen this idea of the oxymoron to the more general term, 'oppositions'. Ask students to look at the first speech we hear from Friar Lawrence: his lines are full of them. Ask them to note each one, beginning with the first line's 'smiles … frowning'.

Now widen this further. Point out that there are contradictions everywhere in this play. There is a binary conflict between two families; another between age and youth. What other conflicts are there everywhere in *Romeo and Juliet*?

The students should talk about this in groups, bearing in mind the opposites in Friar Lawrence's words, and Romeo's and Juliet's oxymorons. They should easily find the obvious opposites – Montague and Capulet; Benvolio the peacemaker and Tybalt 'the fiery' (as Benvolio calls him in 1.1).

One set of oppositions, or contrasts, which the students may not find, appears in the different natures of successive scenes. For example, 1.1 and 1.2 take place in the street and are, in part, noisy. In 1.3, we are in the middle of the peace of Capulet's house. In 1.4, we are back in the street, with Mercutio's wild fantasies, and in 1.5 we are back in the house … In other words, there are opposites of mood and tone on either side of most of the scene breaks.

Other opposites that I have tried to lead students towards on the task sheet are: fast and slow (there is an obvious example in the last line of this scene, with the Friar's both Fatherly and fatherly words to Romeo); and social reasons for marriage, and private ones. Probably the most important pairings are those of life and death; love and hate; light and dark.

Plenary (10 minutes)
Ask the students to find every speech by Romeo's father, Old Montague: there are few. Then ask them to read all the Friar's lines for any fatherly (not just Fatherly) words or phrases.

Glossary
Osier: willow.

Fleckled seems to be an invention of Shakespeare's: a perfect description of light on receding darkness.

This Titan was the sun god who drove his chariot across the sky.

Good morrow, father

1. Make a colour drawing illustrating the first six lines of the Friar's speech. Make grey-haired morning smile, make night frown, show light in checks on the clouds, and make darkness move away like a drunkard. Once again, check some surrealist art online or in the library, and use your drawing as a preparatory sketch for a painting.

2. We see very little of Romeo's father in this play. Bearing this in mind, talk in groups about Romeo and Friar Lawrence and what we see of their relationship. Note all the words and phrases in this scene (2.3) that might be typical of a father to his son.

3. Take it in turns to act the scene, emphasising all the father/son moments with actions – arms on shoulders, for example. Note any parental irritability. 'Wisely and slow, they stumble that run fast' is Friar Lawrence's last line in this scene. Write down Romeo's private thoughts about that advice.

4. 'My ghostly father', Romeo says to the Friar. What has the Friar just said to him? These words were the opening words in the private confession of the church, as in this French poem by Charles of Orleans (1391–1465):

> My ghostly father I me confess
>   First to God and then to you . . .

It captures the beginning of what confessions would have been like in medieval times. Write a poem beginning 'My ghostly father' for one of the following characters at the end of the play, listing all the sins they have committed ('sins of commission', and all the things they might have done to prevent the tragedy but which they didn't ('sins of omission'):

- the Nurse
- the Friar
- Capulet
- Mercutio (brought back to life).

You will need to look through the play for your evidence.

5. Take a sheet of paper – portrait rather than landscape – and divide it vertically into two columns. On the left hand side, write down all of Friar Lawrence's words and phrases that have positive connotations – all of what we might call his 'feel-good' words. Start with 'grey-eyed morn smiles'. On the right hand side, write down all the negative phrases, beginning with 'frowning night'.

6. There are other examples of opposites throughout the play: the constant conflict between age and youth, for example. What other conflicts can you find?

    Each group should take one of these three pairings: life and death; love and hate; light and dark. Now scour the play (possibly for homework) looking for all references. Share them when the group comes back together.

7. Write a short essay on one of these pairings: 'Life and death [for example] in *Romeo and Juliet*'.

36

Mistress minion you

Act 3 Scene 5, lines 149–168: available online and at the end of this book.

Introduction

Much has happened since the last section. Mercutio and Tybalt are dead; Romeo and Juliet are married; Romeo has been banished; now, Capulet has, as we say today, 'lost it', as Juliet prevaricates about 'marrying' Paris.

Aim

The students have an opportunity to act anger; and to see how Shakespeare uses verse to convey the realities of common speech.

Starter (5 minutes)

Act these lines yourself, but keeping your voice low: there are more ways than one to act anger. If it feels comfortable to do so, move around addressing different lines to different students as if each of them were Juliet.

Main phase (45 minutes)

Ask the students to study these lines individually and then in groups. Ask them to make notes on them, not at first about Capulet, but about Juliet: how is she reacting at each point? They should make notes on her facial expressions and her body language at, for example, 'mistress minion', 'Thursday next', 'hurdle thither'.

And how is Lady Capulet reacting? There are two clues to her behaviour: line 140, about the grave, and line 158, where she reproaches her husband.

Now ask the students to concentrate on Capulet's words. The speech is not obscure, once they have realised how angry Capulet is. But to add colour to their thinking, they should know the following:

- 'Minion' means, originally, 'darling'. Capulet uses it to mean something like 'hussy'. This is double-edged in that he is using a pet word as an insult.
- 'Fettle your fine joints' takes its force from its use in preparing a horse.
- A 'hurdle' was a sledged or wheel-drawn trolley used to drag traitors to execution.
- 'Carrion' is 'putrefying flesh'.
- 'Hilding' means 'good-for-nothing'; it was especially used of a useless horse.
- 'Green-sickness' was a disease, chlorosis, mainly suffered by young girls, involving anaemia and irregular periods.

Ask the students to re-write the lines in a language that would be suitable for a soap opera. They can use Capulet's insults in any order they like, as long as they make them into modern English. They might begin

> Don't talk to me in riddles, you precious
> spoilt darling, you waste of space, you carcase
> fit for the birds to eat. Miss High-and-Mighty . . .

and they might, as here, restrict themselves as much as possible, to ten-syllable lines. Sometimes the rhythm of Shakespeare's lines will have seeped into their minds and helped them write loose iambic pentameters.

Plenary (10 minutes)

Glossary: 'chopt-logic': Capulet says that Juliet is using riddles to evade the truth (which she is, being already married). In modern terms, she is blowing smoke over the reality in a desperate hope. Discuss ways in which we might prevaricate like this today in parent–child conversations.

Mistress minion you

Act 3 Scene 5, lines 149–168

1. The image in the line about the hurdle would have spoken to Juliet about a terrible insult in public. Imagine the scene, and draw it: the hurdle, which would have been like a sledge or a large trolley on wheels, with the girl tied on it, the furious father pulling it, the weeping mother following, spectators jeering, the church – and a baffled Friar: he knows Juliet is already married.

2. Or make a head-and-shoulders drawing of Juliet suffering with the 'green-sickness': pale, weak, greenish. In both cases, write the relevant lines on the drawings and commit them (and the lines around them) to memory.

3. These are terrible insults for a father to throw at his child. Look at these words, and find out their meaning: 'minion'; 'fettle'; 'hurdle'; 'carrion'; 'hilding'. In groups, talk about what these insults imply here about what the father thinks (or, rather, feels) about his daughter.

4. Some ways to read these lines:
   - in a vicious whisper throughout
   - in a shout throughout
   - in a voice that zooms high and reaches low at different punctuation marks and line endings.

5. In a larger space, someone should volunteer to take Juliet's part, while other members of the groups all play Capulet. Juliet should sit or kneel in the middle of a circle, while the others should walk round her hurling these lines at her. Juliet should turn her eyes to each speaker, and try to interrupt with any of her lines from this scene: for example, 146–147, 158–159. Each Capulet must make his own decision about how much of Juliet's lines he will let her speak. Another actor, as Lady Capulet, should repeat line 140 whenever there is a gap: 'I would the fool were married to her grave'. Bear this line in mind with its word 'grave' (which is repeated throughout the play) as you study the rest of the script.

   Each group should repeat this exercise with a different person (always a volunteer! And not always a female) each time. They should find the most effective way of staging the passage, and present it to the rest of the class, or, if possible, to another audience.

6. Parental relations

   Why is Capulet so angry? Discuss this in groups. Go beyond 'Because she won't marry Paris'. The words 'authority' and 'honour' might come into your discussion.

   Notice how he throws her words back at her: 'proud', 'I thank you', 'I thank you not', 'not proud'. Think how this happens in violent quarrels in everyday life: Shakespeare's genius is part his ability to put common speech in powerful verse. Note, as well, how Capulet repeats himself. Read his lines again, noting each repetition and each time that he repeats something Juliet has said.

© Fred Sedgwick, 2011. *Resources for Teaching Shakespeare: 11–16.*

37

Take thou this vial

Act 4 Scene 1, lines 78–85 and 93–106: available online and at the end of this book.

Introduction
Romeo and Juliet may be a love story, but it is just as much a death story. The critic M. Mahood comments, 'Death has long been Romeo's rival and enjoys Juliet at the last' (quoted in Harold Bloom, *Shakespeare: The Invention of the Human*).

Aims
The students will appreciate how Death is built up almost as a character; they will begin to see more deeply into Friar Lawrence's character; and they will appreciate the special kind of predicament in which Juliet finds herself.

Starter (5 minutes)
Point out that Juliet's reason for not marrying Paris goes deeper than the reasons some girls might have for not wanting to marry their parents' choice: it's not just that she loves Romeo, but that she is already married to him! In Shakespeare's time, she would be committing a sin that would put her in danger of Hell if she went through with the service at Saint Peter's church. It is easy for the students to forget this in our almost entirely secular age.

Main phase (45 minutes)
Ask the students to play with Juliet's lines to the Friar (77–86). For example, a different student might read each experience Juliet is prepared to undergo rather than marry Paris. They should make their readings as chilling as possible.

Point out that Death is practically a character in this play, as the quotation from Mahood suggests. In the Friar's speech online, Death has a capital – and is called 'he', not 'it'. Ask the students to divide the play up amongst themselves in groups, and to count every reference to death and associated words and ideas, such as 'grave', 'kill', 'tomb', etc. They should include words less obviously death-oriented: 'sped', for example, meaning to die quickly. They may need to be told that 'corse' means 'corpse'. Direct them especially to the conversation between Juliet and the Nurse at 3.2, lines 97–137, where 'death' and associated words occur nearly 20 times.

Make sure also that the students come across Capulet's lines in 4.3.36–40: Death has 'lain' with Juliet; Death is Capulet's 'son-in-law'. Recall Lady Capulet's line, 'I would the fool were married to her grave' (3.5.140).

They should make a note of each reference, and its context. I have given an example on the task sheet; it would be helpful if you could offer one yourself – for example, the way death is mentioned often in the first act, as if to prepare us for a less than happy ending to the love story. It is even mentioned, very solemnly, by the very young Juliet several times (1.5, line 134, for example) and in 2.2, line 64. Once again, the tragic ending of the play is foreshadowed by one of its victims.

Plenary (10 minutes)
If the students have brainstormed words about the character of the Friar (see question 5 on the task sheet), write them up. Some suggestions you might add to the mix are 'fatherly', 'loquacious', 'verbose', 'preachy', 'dangerous' (another possible oxymoron here: a dangerous father!), 'dodgy', 'druggy', etc.

Discuss how the Friar should be played.

Glossary
Charnel-house: a building in a graveyard where bones were stacked.
Surcease: end.

Take thou this vial

Act 4 Scene 1, lines 78–85 and 93–106

1. Read Juliet's lines about what she would rather do than marry Paris. Using dark materials – charcoal, perhaps – make a drawing to illustrate one of the lines, and write that line on the drawing as a title. Make sure you know what 'shanks' and 'chaps' are. If you have studied *Macbeth*, you should find a reference to chaps very early in that play.

2. Juliet is desperate not to marry Paris. This is because she loves Romeo, of course. But there is another reason. Find out what sin she would be committing if she were to go through with the service at Saint Peter's Church. Remember that this play, which has many religious references, was written at a time when everyone went to church and believed in eternal damnation.

3. When you have studied Juliet's lines (77–86), write a modern version: a girl says all the things she'd rather do than marry the wrong man (or marry a man when she is already secretly married to her lover). Make your lines suitable for a television drama.

4. Read these lines of Juliet's again several times until you know them off by heart. Now take turns to act them as dramatically as possible. You could read them solo, or with each group member reading a different experience that Juliet would prefer to the marriage.

5. What kind of person is the Friar? Brainstorm some words you might use to describe him.
   Note these points:
   - the tone of his words to Romeo and Juliet
   - the length of his speeches
   - the fact that he encourages Juliet to tell her parents a lie (find this lie).

6. Read the whole of the Friar's speech in groups, changing readers at every punctuation mark. Pause. Mime what he is saying Juliet must do at each of his instructions. Make sure you have fully understood all that he is saying, and discuss him and his instructions.

7. Death and death
   When you examine the play looking for references for Death – or death – make sure that you count all associated words. Note each reference, and put it in its context. Note, for example:
   - Who referred to death (or Death)?
   - To whom were they talking?
   - What is the effect of that reference?

   For example, in 1.5, Juliet says to the Nurse: 'If he be married / My grave is like to be my wedding bed'. Thus she unwittingly anticipates both her own pretended death and her real one; later, the Chorus between Acts 1 and 2 echoes this in the first line: 'Now old desire doth in his death-bed lie'. And these repetitions are spoken before anyone – Mercutio or Tybalt – have died.

   Chose two other death references and make notes on them like these.

38

Farewell! God knows when we shall meet again

Act 4 Scene 3, lines from Juliet's speech 14–58: available online and at the end of this book.

Introduction

Juliet's tomb. This is one of the big moments in Shakespeare. It is a moment which some of the students will keep in their memories and be forever grateful to us if we can teach it vividly.

Aims

Students will appreciate the drama of Juliet' situation. They will see how Shakespeare anticipates modern horror films. They also will appreciate the way in which feeling can be locked inside technique, in this case, the young Shakespeare's iambic pentameters.

Starter (5 minutes)

Introduce, or re-introduce, the idea of soliloquy. If the students have studied *Macbeth* and *A Midsummer Night's Dream*, you could recall Macbeth's soliloquy in the dagger scene (2.1) and Bottom's lines on his awakening from his 'bottomless dream' (4.1). Point out that this is another soliloquy in iambic pentameters. You could use the technique in *A Midsummer Night's Dream* Chapter 19 to introduce the metre of this line here, or work through part 5 on the task sheet.

Main phase (45 minutes)

The students will readily see that this soliloquy is divided into an introduction ('Farewell!' onwards) and five other sections, each beginning in the same way: with a phrase containing the word 'if', and detailing a dread. Ask the students in groups to speak the whole speech in different ways. They might do this in one of the following ways:

- allot the introduction and each fear to a different student
- speak the words, changing speaker at various (not all, though) punctuation marks.
- Or (most dramatically) they might arrange all the students in the class in a circle. Each student should speak one line, and then turn to a colleague who should carry on the speech. With this way of saying the lines, the students should note that in each section, Juliet's fear is greater than in the previous one. They should convey in their reading a sense of mounting terror.

Before they give their version of the lines, point out that while over-the-top, hammy acting is out of order in a production on the stage or on television or film, it is likely that the actors have gone through a stage of overdoing things. They should, therefore, at this stage, not being afraid to give full vent to their version of Juliet's feelings in the lines.

Ask the students to learn by heart either the introduction or one of the fear sections.

Plenary (10 minutes)

Ask the students to research the mandrake (line 47). This was a plant that was believed to grow underneath gibbets. It shrieked when it was pulled up. It is believed that the name is a Latinised version of Sanskrit *mandros* 'sleep' and *agora* 'substance'; so it is apt that Juliet mentions it here.

Farewell! God knows when we shall meet again

Act 4 Scene 3, lines from Juliet's speech 14–58

1 This soliloquy is constructed like this: there is an introduction, and then five sections, each beginning with a phrase with the word 'if' in it. Most of us have times when we are worried, and anticipate fearfully like this (though not, it must be hoped, while facing such a terrible situation as Juliet's). Make a note of what each fear is in your own words, and share your findings.

2 Draw one of Juliet's fears as vividly as possible. There are plenty of images in the lines to make suitably disturbing images: the dagger, Juliet's own dead body and her ancestors' bones, the stifling vault, 'the mangled Tybalt in his shroud' . . .

3 Make drawings for the other fears, and make a short manga book with six pages (the first for the 'Farewell!' introduction, and one for each of the fears). Or make a single cartoon page of the six drawings on a smaller scale.

   Or you could draw each dread of Juliet's as a still from a horror film.

4 At one point, Shakespeare has Juliet beginning to talk to herself about a fear that she can't bring herself to describe. Identify where this happens, and then write down that fear. You could try to do this in Shakespearean language, or in modern language.

5 Iambic pentameters

   Leonardo da Vinci, the great Renaissance artist, wrote that 'we have to imprison art in order to make it free'. The terror Juliet feels in this situation comes across to us all the more powerfully because Shakespeare imprisons Juliet's words in iambic pentameters.

   The following example will help you to get a grasp of all Shakespearean verse. In an iambic pentameter, each line has ten syllables (though sometimes there will be an extra one or two, or one or two fewer). Each pair of syllables is called an *iamb*, which means 'foot'. So each line has five feet (two syllables in each one). And each foot is made up of a weak unaccented syllable (the first), and a strong accented one (the second):

   a**LACK** a**LACK** is **IT** not **LIKE** that **I**

   or

   to**ge**ther **with** the **sor**row **of** this **place**

It is important to note that, though many of the lines (like the second one above) do not follow the rules exactly, the line arranged in fives like this is the essential beat of Shakespeare's verse.

6 A near-contemporary of Shakespeare's, the poet John Donne, began a love poem composed of impossible things:

> Go, and catch a falling star,
> Get with child a mandrake root

Combine your research on mandrakes and your close reading of Juliet's speech, and write a horror poem. Here is an example of a beginning:

> I heard the mandrake scream and drank . . .

7 A modern poet, T. S. Eliot, has a line in his poem 'Portrait of a Lady' which describes a room with 'An atmosphere of Juliet's tomb'. Write a piece of prose or a poem using the ideas in Juliet's speech. Eliot's line could be your title.

39

She's dead, deceased, dead

Act 4 Scene 5, lines 19–33: available online and at the end of this book.

Introduction and aims

In this dramatic scene, Shakespeare provides an opportunity for the students to examine further the characters of the Nurse and Juliet's parents, and to see how Shakespeare writes when his characters are in shock.

Starter (5 minutes)

Ask two students to read lines 15–24 between Lady Capulet and the Nurse. Ask them to exaggerate what appears to be hysteria. Ask them to note how Lady Capulet repeats some of the Nurse's words.

Main phase (45 minutes)

Ask the students in pairs to prepare a mini radio play of those lines. Then ask them to prepare a play with actions. Finally, every pair should share their versions.

Now ask each group of students to read Capulet's speeches beginning 'Hah, let me see her' and 'Ready to go', swapping speakers at line endings or punctuation marks. Ask them to work in groups to find words that describe the differences between the ways the mother and the servant, on the one hand, have reacted to Juliet's apparent death, and the father on the other.

Ask them to read all the Nurse's lines in the play since the beginning of Act 2, and to write down individually some words that might describe how her character appears in these scenes. Ask them to share their findings in groups. Then ask them to concentrate on this scene – not just the lines given online, but everything from line 1 ('Mistress, what mistress!') to the entry of Friar Lawrence. What do we learn about the Nurse here?

On the task sheet, the students have been asked to think about lines 23–24 where Lady Capulet and the Nurse wail immediately after the discovery of Juliet's body, and to suggest ways of speaking them that the actors might use to prevent the possibility of laughter. Some suggestions might be:

- Make them indecipherable (as indeed words spoken in shock often are).
- Speak them so that only the essential words are audible.
- Speak them very fast, the two actors almost covering each other's lines.
- Speak them, counter-intuitively, quietly, in stage whispers.
- Make the Nurse and Lady Capulet speak them in different ways.
- Cut them.

Plenary (5 minutes)

Ask if Capulet's words at lines 30–32 do not contradict themselves – is this a clue about his character? Ask two students to read the lines as strongly as they can. Another clue to Capulet might be his line 'Death . . . hath tane her hence to make me wail'. She's died to make him cry?

Ask about the Friar. How does he enter? Discuss: What does he know that the others don't? How should he speak this line? – and also his lines at 65 onwards where he lies and lies?

She's dead, deceased, dead

Act 4 Scene 5, lines 19–33

1 'Death lies on her like an untimely frost / Upon the sweetest flower of the field'. This simile is an extended one. The basic sense is that death is a frost: a dead person becomes white. But it is also an 'untimely' frost, because Juliet is so young. And it lies upon 'the sweetest flower'.

   Write your own extended similes for death, using Mercutio and Tybalt as starting points. For example, you might write for Mercutio:

   Death is like a curse full of plague and sickness on two houses.

   When you have done this, convert your similes into metaphors, or write metaphors for the characters.

   • For Mercutio, for example: Death is an end to all Queen Mab and lechery.
     or
   • It is a sly stab under a friend's arm.

2 Write similes and metaphors that would suit this play about other subjects. They can be in Shakespearean or in modern language:

   • Love
   • The Nurse
   • A tomb
   • The Friar.

3 Read the Nurse's speech at the beginning of this scene. Do this in groups, experimenting with different ways of saying it. First, you might vary the speed: the early lines seem to need to be spoken very fast. Where would you slow down?

4 Imagine you are rehearsing this play, and someone says that two of the lines are way over the top, and to demonstrate speaks them in a shriek that might suit a comedy show: 'She's dead, deceased, she's dead, alack the day! / Alack the day, she's dead, she's dead, she's dead!' Everyone laughs.

   What is your reaction? Above all, you need to try to make sure that the audience doesn't laugh . . .

   Think of ways the lines might be said.

5 Look at lines 25–28. Read the speech, changing speakers at each full stop and exclamation mark. Share your reading with the rest of the class. Then ask yourselves, what kind of man is Capulet? Go through the play, noting all his speeches, and make notes about how you would advise an actor to portray him.

6 'Her lord'. In a scene like this, this might seem trivial. But many productions of the play, especially in recent years, have put an emphasis on how Juliet, representing other young people, is treated by her father. Discuss how you would feel as a girl hearing your father announce your future husband as 'your lord'.

   Make a list of words that describe how Juliet is treated by her father throughout the play.

40

Who calls so loud?

Act 5 Scene 1, lines 57–75: available online and at the end of this book.

Introduction

Although this scene depicts Romeo and the Apothecary, it also presents an opportunity to compare and contrast the characters of Romeo and Juliet.

Aims

During this session students will consolidate their understanding of the two leading characters of the play; think about ways in which the Apothecary might be played; and reflect on the part that fate (represented by the stars) plays.

Starter (5 minutes)

Sum up the plot between the last section and this one. Since the last scene, Juliet has been presumed dead by her family. In 5.1, moments before his conversation with the Apothecary, Romeo also hears that Juliet is 'dead', and decides to kill himself in Juliet's tomb.

Main phase (45 minutes)

Romeo's character throughout the play

Ask the students, first as individuals, and then in groups, to read everything Romeo has said throughout the play so far. They should note how he relates to other characters: to Benvolio, to Mercutio, to Juliet (of course), to Friar Lawrence, to Tybalt – what does he say to them, and how do they respond?

Ask them, in groups (possibly sharing out the acts between them and then pooling their findings) to find words that describe his character, noting down both the references and some comments on those references. For example, in 1.1, the Romeo that Benvolio talks to is a loner, self-pitying, possibly immature: 'Ay me, sad hours seem long' (line 154). Other possible words are: changeable, impulsive, religious; but there are many others.

Given the words that they come up with, and the fact that a few moments before this conversation with the Apothecary, Romeo has heard the worst of all possible news, the students should think about ways of speaking his lines. Then, in twos, they should act the lines for a radio play. They should consider: how do we want this man to come across to the audience?

They should read everything Juliet has said throughout the play so far, and compare her with Romeo.

Then ask them in groups to discuss: Who seems to be the stronger, the more mature character? Who makes things happen? If they had survived, what would they have been like as a middle-aged couple?

Ask the students to act this scene between Romeo and the Apothecary. Tell them that Shakespeare's friend Ben Jonson wrote that Shakespeare was 'for all time'; that a famous book is called *Shakespeare our Contemporary*. There are some lines that strike a modern note here. Ask them to discuss what these are. Romeo pushes the Apothecary into acting as a fixer. 'Gear' seems especially in place.

Plenary (10 minutes)

The stars figure largely in the play. Ask the students, possibly for homework, to find every reference to them. Begin by reading Romeo's response to the news of Juliet's supposed death (line 24). Ask them to discuss what the stars stand for here – and also for some people today who trust horoscopes.

Who calls so loud?

Act 5 Scene 1, lines 57–75

1 Imagine that you are helping to produce the play in modern dress. Advise the director on possible ways of dressing the Apothecary. First, draw him, keeping close to Romeo's description. The keywords are in lines 58, 68–69 and 70–74. Make notes under your drawing, describing your costume: materials, colours, state of repair and anything else that is relevant. Compare your drawings with each other.

2 What trader in modern times does the Apothecary most remind you of? In one production he was a fixer. In another, he was silently on stage throughout the play, like a guardian of fate: in this production, he always knew what was going to happen. Chose a scene from the play, and imagine that you are in this production, playing the Apothecary. How do you react at different points? With grim satisfaction? With sad resignation? With sick hilarity? Some examples:
   * when the servants brawl at the very beginning
   * when the lovers meet at the Capulets' ball (the 'palmer' speech)
   * when Mercutio, and later Tybalt are killed
   * when the Friar offers to help Romeo
   * when Capulet screams abuse at his daughter.

3 Spend a long time on Romeo's lines throughout the play. Do this first on your own, and then share your findings. What sort of person is he? Produce evidence for your answers to this question. Do the same with Juliet.

   Then, fold a large sheet of paper vertically in half. Write Romeo at the top of one half, and Juliet at the top of the other. Fill the sheet with your findings.

4 Look at Romeo's lines from 'And that the trunk . . .' to 'cannon's womb'. Look again at Chapter 39, and revise your work on similes and metaphors. Note that these lines contain both a simile and metaphor; the metaphor is genuinely frightening. Work out which is the simile and which the metaphor, and discuss them in groups.

5 'I do defy you, stars!' The stars figure in this play from the very beginning. They stand for fate (as the Apothecary did in the production above). Find the moments when the lovers refer to them. One central theme of the play is a pair of opposites that you can think of in many ways: free will and fate, a person's actions and those of the stars. At one point in 1.5, Romeo seems to suggest that God directs his life. Find this line.

   In Shakespeare's most famous play, Hamlet says 'There's a divinity that shapes our ends'. On the other hand, the Victorian poet W. E. Henley wrote: 'I am the master of my fate: / I am the captain of my soul'.

   Write a short article referring to *Romeo and Juliet* called either 'A divinity shapes our ends' or 'We are the masters / mistresses of our fates'. In groups, share your views.

41

O Brother Montague

Act 5 Scene 3, lines 296–310: available online and at the end of this book.

Introduction

This section is about several aspects of Act 5 Scene 3.

Aims

The students will see yet more light shed on Romeo; they will reflect further on fate as a central idea in the play; and they will ask questions about the sincerity of Montague's and Capulet's final words.

They will also see how Shakespeare sketches characters with a few strokes: in this scene, Paris, the Captain and the Prince.

Starter (15 minutes)

Read, or rather act, the Friar's long speech from line 239 onwards. Raise some questions with the students: are the first four words a joke on Shakespeare's part? Should the speech be cut altogether, or shortened? If the latter, which parts might be cut? Or does the complete speech serve a purpose?

Ask the students to look for the religious language we might expect. There is none, of course. Raise the question of why the Friar's tone has changed. Presumably, Shakespeare intends to present a nervous man before his social superiors in a supremely delicate situation in which, moreover, he might be thought to bear some responsibility.

Main phase (40 minutes)

Clear pictures emerge here of aspects of the characters of both Paris and Romeo. The ideas on the task sheet are aimed at enabling the students to see, first, how peremptory Paris is in his dealing with his servant and, second, how falsely his words to Juliet ring. Third, they will see how the nervous violence that affects Romeo's language adds to what they already know of this storm-driven, religious character.

The central speech in the scene is Romeo's (lines 74 onwards). It divides into seven parts: his first reflection, his first set of words to Juliet, his words to Paris, his words to Tybalt, his second set of words to Juliet; his resolve; and his talking of the poison. In groups, students should practise ways of acting these lines: changing speakers at punctuation marks, for example.

Images of the sea, and sea journeys occur frequently in Romeo's speech. Here are some of the references:

- 1.1.183: Love is, among other things, 'a sea nourished with loving tears'.
- 1.4.112: Romeo prays to 'He that hath the steerage of my course'.
- 2.2.82ff: Romeo says he is 'no pilot' and goes on to talk about 'the farthest sea'.
- 5.3.39: He will, he says, be 'more fierce . . . than the roaring sea'.
- 5.3.118: In his last words, he compares himself to 'a seasick weary bark'.

The effect is to paint a picture of a rudderless young man.

Plenary (5 minutes)

Point out how Shakespeare gives glimpses of even minor characters: the Captain's pun on 'ground' for example, tells us something about him; and students might ask themselves whether the Prince's 'I told you so!' tone at lines 291–295, and his heartless remark to Montague at line 209 are a sensitive as they might be.

Glossary

A jointure is a sum of money settled by the bridegroom's father on the bride.

O Brother Montague

Act 5 Scene 3, lines 296–310

1. Make a drawing of the scene as it is at line 21: Paris hides, and Romeo and Balthazar enter with a mattock, a torch and a crowbar ('wrenching iron'). Capture in your drawing the gloom of a churchyard, the brightness of the torch and the details of the tools. A mattock was an agricultural tool, a kind of combined axe and pick. It was used to loosen hard ground and to grub up trees.

2. Paris' character
   Count his orders to the Page in his first speech. Now, in twos, take turns to read these lines as sharply as possible while the other reacts as his Page.

   Look carefully at the language of Paris' last words to Juliet (almost a partial sonnet interrupted by the boy's whistle). Read them, trying to sound sincere. In groups, try other ways of reading them. Which ways suits them best?

3. Romeo's language
   In groups, read Romeo's speech beginning 'Give me that mattock'. Make sure that your reading reflects the meaning of the words, especially when he threatens Balthazar. Change readers at each punctuation mark. Discuss: Why does he lie to his servant?

   The sea stands for something to Romeo. Find all the references Romeo makes to it. The main ones are in Acts 1 and 5. Think about what this adds to our knowledge of him as a character, and discuss your findings in groups.

4. In groups, act the last five speeches of the play. Think of adverbs to describe how Capulet and Montague react to the Prince and say their own lines. There are more possibilities than you might think at first. Some options are:
   - sincerely
   - unhopefully
   - dubiously
   - sarcastically
   - cynically.

   Note the words 'jointure' and 'gold'. Sum up as best you can in discussion: what are the fathers' immediate ideas for making amends to each other for the death of the lovers?

5. Why did Romeo and Juliet die? Discuss the possibilities below in groups. Each group should try to settle on one or more of these, and be prepared to give reasons for their choice to the whole class:
   - their own stupidity
   - the Friar's mistake
   - a bad postal service
   - their violent society
   - their stiff unbending parents
   - fate.

6. Puns: in the first section, there are examples of Shakespeare's fondness for wordplay – not, as today, just for the sake of a joke. Find Mercutio's grim pun that he makes as he lies dying. A character in this tragic scene also puns.

7. Write an obituary for one of the lovers, describing their character, backing up your points with quotations from the play.

A note on prose and verse

Once we have made sure that the students know how to distinguish between verse and prose on the page, they may need some historical background. It will seem strange to students familiar with television, drama and films, but all Ancient Greek and Roman plays were written in verse, and verse was still the main medium for plays in Shakespeare's time. Indeed, Shakespeare was ahead of his time in mixing the two media.

An exercise will help students to understand the different functions of prose on the one hand and verse on the other. Ask the students to find the only scenes in, for example, *Macbeth*, that are in prose. They are: Lady Macbeth reading the letter (1.5); the Porter scene (2.3); some of Macbeth's conversation with the murderers in 3.1; and the sleep-walking scene 5:1.

Discuss with them the difference between verse and prose in this play with particular reference to these statements:

- Shakespeare was, of course, a poet, and the big moments are given in verse: the great dagger speech, for example in 2.1.
- It is a class thing: the lower classes use prose, the upper class use verse. There are three exceptions to this rule in the play, when an aristocratic character speaks in prose. Ask the students to find them, and suggest reasons for this. They are Macbeth's words to the murderers, the Macbeths' few words at the beginning of this scene, Lady Macbeth reading a letter, and later, in her madness (perhaps mad people can't frame verse . . .).
- Classical drama was always in verse until Shakespeare's time.

Keywords and key themes in Shakespeare plays

The keywords in the three main plays dealt with in this book emerge in the task sheets. To summarise, *Macbeth* has not so much keywords as key *ideas* – that of opposites, apparent contradictions or, to use the Porter's word, equivocations. Also, babies are central to the play's imagery, signifying innocence and vulnerability, and the importance to Macbeth and Macduff of dynasty. And this last idea is linked to time: note that the first word of the play is 'When'.

Romeo and Juliet plays with obscenity from the first scene and, as Eric Partridge writes (in *Shakespeare's Bawdy*) 'Mercutio and the Nurse sex-spatter the most lyrically tragic of the plays'. This provides a contrasting back projection to the foreground love story. Again, the play is full of oppositions, often in the form of oxymorons. There are many points at which students of this play could be referred to *Macbeth*. 'Fiend angelical' (*Romeo and Juliet*) as a phrase has much in common with 'Fair is foul' (*Macbeth*).

A Midsummer Night's Dream plays with the idea of discord – between husband-to-be and wife-to-be, between king and queen, between father and daughter and, memorably, between elements of nature in Titania's great speech in 2.1, where we read about climate change, no less. That the course of true love does not, indeed, run smooth is prefigured by the news that Theseus courted his new bride with his sword: his is a political marriage, and the love he expresses is merely expedient.

Brief notes on other plays

Henry IV Part 1

This play is about contrasts: between the Prince, who, the King thinks, has dishonoured himself with his friends at the tavern, and Hotspur; and between order and disorder (the latter is presented to us in the first line of the play). The play is also about contrasting views of honour: a cynical view is summed up by the words and actions of Falstaff; a medieval view by the words and actions of Hotspur.

Henry V

Landscape and horticulture figure prominently: 'strawberries' and 'honey-bees' are images used by the churchmen in Act 1; the constable of France compares the young prince Hal to roots hidden underneath filth. Often the images are of fields gone to seed. Movingly (the Hostess tells us), Falstaff 'babbled of green fields' as he died. At the end of the play Burgundy has an extended metaphor of France as 'the best garden of the world . . . Corrupting in its own fertility'.

King Lear

We are left in no doubt from early on about the importance of the word 'nothing' and other negatives. This usage climaxes in Lear's line in 5.3, 'Never, never, never, never, never.' An early exchange between Lear and Kent (1.1) signals another preoccupation: seeing and blindness: 'LEAR: Out of my sight! KENT: See better, Lear.' This opposition is terribly enacted in Gloucester's blinding. Nearly every character appeals to nature – and the way each character understands nature is a central theme.

Richard III

This play is full of animal imagery. Eagles, kites, buzzards, wolves, spiders, toads, dogs, hedgehogs – all are mentioned in the first two scenes, and Richard himself, whose crest was a wild boar, is frequently compared unfavourably to members of the pig family. Lord Hastings talks about wild birds in 1.1.133–134: 'More pity that the eagles should be mewed / While kites and buzzards play at liberty'.

Acting is another theme. From the beginning of this play, Richard is not only an actor, but aware that he is one. Indeed, he tells us so: in his first speech he says that because he is not built by nature to play the part of the lover (though he does, of course, straightaway: more acting) he will play the part of the villain. His courting of Anne is an impressive, repellent – and ultimately convincing act. He acts in 1.3, 'I am too childish-foolish for this world'.

The Tempest

There is more music in this play than in any other Shakespeare play: the isle is, indeed, 'full of noises'. Nature is prominent, especially the sea and the air, but also the earth and its flora.

Twelfth Night

Madness: nobody in this play acts completely sanely, and Malvolio is almost driven mad by his treatment at the hands of Belch and Feste and the others.

Films

What follows is a list of films of the three main plays dealt with in this book, with notes. All are available on DVD.

Macbeth

One recommended DVD is Roman Polanski's 1971 film, starring Jon Finch and Francesca Annis (both too young for their parts, especially Annis at 25). Most of the violence that occurs off-stage in the play is shown on screen, and there is unscripted violence: a gratuitous stabbing of a dying man sets the tone in the first few minutes, and we see the deaths of two of Banquo's murderers (thus Polanski underlines the enormity of Macbeth's tyranny: he'll kill his own henchmen to feel safer). This film is useful with students, partly because the violence of the poetry is underscored by the imagery. It is one of the rare productions that shows Banquo's ghost as a physical entity rather than as an absence: a topic for discussion.

Also recommended is a DVD of a Trevor Nunn production. He directed the play with the Royal Shakespeare Company, and the production was filmed by Thames Television in 1978. Ian McKellen and Judi Dench star. This version is claustrophobic and shot close-up, and McKellen and Dench are all too watchable: the latter is genuinely frightening in her early soliloquies, where she even scares herself into retching. Students will benefit, not only from seeing the whole play in this version, but even more perhaps, by studying it scene by scene; especially those scenes where the Macbeths are alone together. Students will be surprised at the doubling of parts, which is fine on stage; but which jars a little on screen. At one point the drunken porter turns up as a lord.

A Midsummer Night's Dream

There are, again, two recommended versions. Adrian Noble directed the play for the Royal Shakespeare Company, and this production was filmed by Channel 4 (2001). It introduces a new character, a modern little boy in pyjamas. This works when we see the action unfold, as if through his eyes. Alex Jennings doubles as Theseus and Oberon, and Lindsay Duncan as Hyppolita and Titania; but this isn't because of a small company, but to emphasise parallels between the duke and the king of the fairies on the one hand, and Hyppolita and Titania on the other. There is some doubt about the royal marriage from the start, especially when Hyppolita cuffs Theseus for his treatment of Hermia. The fairies and the mechanicals (except for Bottom, who is pivotal to the scene) are also doubled.

Jonathan Miller's production for the BBC, which dates from 1981, is worth watching because, like all these productions, it is almost completely uncut.

Both these productions make it clear that Titania and Bottom have sex. I think this raises an issue that might be explored: is it in Oberon's nature to let this happen? Is it in his interest?

Romeo and Juliet

Baz Luhrmann's *Romeo + Juliet* (Twentieth Century Fox, 1996). The remarkable thing about this terrific film is how, despite being streetwise beyond the bounds of what might have been thought possible, it uses Shakespeare's words, albeit drastically cut. From the prologue, delivered as a newscast, to the end, it is utterly convincing, with superb performances by Claire Danes and Leonardo DiCaprio. It's recommended for any point in the students' studies, but would be a brilliant kickstart for them. It has to be said that sometimes the pace of the speech, the American accents and the background music make it unintelligible to some ears.

In the BBC production of 1978 there is the young Alan Rickman as a sneering Tybalt, and a wonderful death from Andrew Anthony's camp Mercutio. But the lovers are less strongly played. As with all these BBC productions from the late seventies, almost the whole text is there.

Further reading

Reference

A dictionary with etymological roots is very helpful in any classroom: it will so often shed light on words like 'dote' in *A Midsummer Night's Dream* and 'equivocation' in *Macbeth*. The *Collins English Dictionary* (2006) or *The Chambers Dictionary* (9th edn, 2003) are both excellent. Pocket dictionaries, and the usual 'school' dictionaries offer no help in this way.

Two other reference books are invaluable: a large thesaurus – again, not one designed for schools, but a full one such as the *Bloomsbury Thesaurus* (ed. Fran Alexander, 1997); and Martin Gray's *Dictionary of Literary Terms* (Longman, 1984).

Other

Harold Bloom (1999) *Shakespeare: The Invention of the Human*. London: Fourth Estate. Bloom often overstates his case, but his enthusiasm is infectious. He is especially good on Bottom, whom he sees as 'shrewd . . . kind . . . admirable . . . There is no darkness in Bottom'.

Michael Dobson, general editor, and Stanley Wells, associate general editor (2001) *The Oxford Companion to Shakespeare*. Oxford: Oxford University Press. This is a precious resource for the classroom, and the keener students will gain much information from it.

Rex Gibson (1998) *Teaching Shakespeare*. Cambridge: Cambridge University Press. This is full of good sense and excellent teaching ideas.

Ted Hughes (1997) *Tales from Ovid: Twenty-four Passages from the* Metamorphoses. London: Faber. Shakespeare had read the first century Roman poet Ovid, whose great poem shows an obsession with the way everything changes. It is an influence behind *A Midsummer Night's Dream*, and Ted Hughes' versions are accessible and powerful.

Frank Kermode (2000) *Shakespeare's Language*. London: Penguin. This book asserts the importance of Shakespeare the poet. Kermode believes that this aspect of the plays has 'dropped out of consideration'.

Benedict Nightingale (2010) 'Great Moments in the Theatre: McKellan's *Macbeth*', *The Times*, 21 May, 2010.

Eric Partridge (1947) *Shakespeare's Bawdy*. London: Routledge.

Daniel Rosenthal (2000) *Shakespeare on Screen*. London: Hamlyn. Alongside Dobson and Wells (above) and Wells (below), a useful classroom resource.

Royal Shakespeare Company (2010) *The RSC Shakespeare Toolkit for Teachers*. London: Methuen.

Fred Sedgwick (1999) *Shakespeare and the Young Writer*. London: Routledge.

Stanley Wells (2002) *Shakespeare for All Time*. London: Macmillan.

The play editions that I recommend for secondary school students are all published by the Cambridge University Press (general editor: Rex Gibson).

Macbeth, ed. Rex Gibson (1993).

A Midsummer Night's Dream, ed. Linda Buckle and Paul Kelly (1992).

Romeo and Juliet, ed. Rex Gibson (1992).

The RSC editions are useful for their introductions by Jonathan Bate and for comments by directors on Shakespeare in performance. They are all edited by Bate and Eric Rasmussen, and published by Macmillan. The *Midsummer Night's Dream* edition was published in 2008, and *Macbeth* and *Romeo and Juliet* in 2009. Sometimes the act and scene numbers differ from those in the Cambridge series.

Extracts from plays

Section 1: *Macbeth*

1 Lost and won

Act 1 Scene 1, lines 1–11

> *Thunder and lightning. Enter* THREE WITCHES
>
> FIRST WITCH: When shall we three meet again?
> In thunder, lightning, or in rain?
>
> SECOND WITCH: When the hurly-burly's done,
> When the battle's lost and won.
>
> THIRD WITCH: That will be ere the set of sun.
>
> FIRST WITCH: Where the place?
>
> SECOND WITCH: Upon the heath.
>
> THIRD WITCH: There to meet with Macbeth.
>
> FIRST WITCH: I come, Graymalkin.
>
> SECOND WITCH: Paddock calls.
>
> THIRD WITCH: Anon.
>
> ALL: Fair is foul, and foul is fair,
>   Hover through the fog and filthy air.

2 Killing machine

Act 1 Scene 2, especially lines 7–23

> CAPTAIN: Doubtful it stood,
> As two spent swimmers that do cling together
> And choke their art. The merciless Macdonald –
> Worthy to be a rebel, for to that
> The multiplying villainies of nature
> Do swarm upon him – from the Western Isles
> Of kerns and galloglasses is supplied,
> And fortune on his damned quarrel smiling,
> Showed like a rebel's whore. But all's weak,
> For brave Macbeth – well he deserves that name –
> Disdaining Fortune, with his brandished steel
> Which smoked with bloody execution,
> Like Valour's minion carved out his passage
> Till he faced the slave,
> Which ne'er shook hands, nor bade farewell to him,
> Till he unseamed him from the nave to the chaps
> And fixed his head upon our battlements.

3 The milk of human kindness

Act 1 Scene 5, selected lines from 'They met me' to 'murd'ring ministers'

LADY MACBETH [*reads*]: 'They met me in the day of my success, and I have learned by the perfectest report that they have more in them than mortal knowledge. When I burned in desire to question them further, they made themselves air, into which they vanished. Whiles I stood rapt in the wonder of it, came missives from the king, who all-hailed me Thane of Cawdor, by which title these weird sisters saluted me and referred me to the coming on of time, with "Hail, king that shalt be". This I have thought to deliver thee, my dearest partner of greatness, that thou mightst not lose the dues of rejoicing by being ignorant of what greatness is promised thee . . .'

. . .

    I do fear thy nature,
It is too full o'th'milk of human kindness
To catch the nearest way. Thou wouldst be great,
Art not without ambition, but without
The illness should attend it. What thou wouldst highly,
That wouldst thou holily; wouldst not play false,
And yet wouldst wrongly win . . .

    Hie thee hither,
That I may pour my spirits in thine ear . . .

. . .

The raven himself is hoarse . . .

. . .

    Come, you spirits
That tend on mortal thoughts, unsex me here
And fill me from the crown to the toe topfull
Or direst cruelty; make thick my blood,
Stop th'access and passage to remorse . . .
Come to my woman's breasts
And take my milk for gall, you murd'ring ministers . . .

4 A pleasant seat

Act 1 Scene 6, lines 1–14

DUNCAN: This castle hath a pleasant seat; the air
Nimbly and sweetly recommends itself
Unto our gentle senses.

BANQUO: This guest of summer,
The temple-haunting martlet, does approve . . .
               This bird
Hath made his pendent bed and procreant cradle;
Where they most breed and haunt, I have observed
The air is delicate.

[*Enter* LADY MACBETH]

DUNCAN: See, see, our honoured hostess. – The love
That follows us sometime is our trouble,
Which still we thank as love. Herein I teach you

How you shall bid God yield us for your pains
And thank us for your trouble.

LADY MACBETH: All our service,
In every point twice done and then done double,
Were poor and single business to contend
Against those honours deep and broad wherewith
Your majesty loads our house . . .

5   'Twere well it were done quickly

Act 1 Scene 7, lines 1–28

MACBETH: If it were done when 'tis done, then 'twere well
It were done quickly. If th'assassination
Could trammel up the consequence and catch
With his surcease, success, but that this blow
Might be the be-all and the end-all – here,
But here, upon this bank and shoal of time
We'd jump the life to come. But in these cases,
We still have judgement here that we but teach
Bloody instructions, which being taught, return
To plague the inventor. This even-handed justice
Commends th'ingredience of our poisoned chalice
To our own lips. He's here in double trust:
First, as I am his kinsman and his subject,
Strong both against the deed; then, as his host,
Who should against his murderer shut the door,
Not bear the knife myself. Besides, this Duncan
Hath borne his faculties so meek, hath been
So clear in his great office, that his virtues
Will plead like angels, trumpet-tongued against
The deep damnation of his taking off.
And pity, like a naked new-born babe
Striding the blast, or heaven's cherubim horsed
Upon the sightless couriers of the air,
Shall blow the horrid deed in every eye . . .

6   I have given suck

Act 1 Scene 7, lines 35–41, 46 and 48–59

LADY MACBETH: Was the hope drunk
Wherein you dressed yourself? Hath it slept since?
And wakes it now to look so green and pale
At what it did so freely? From this time,
Such I account thy love. Art thou afeard
To be the same in thine own act and valour,
As thou art in desire?

. . .

MACBETH: I dare do all that may become a man . . .

LADY MACBETH
        What beast was't then

That made you break this enterprise to me?
When you durst do it, then you were a man.
And to be more than what you were, you would
Be so much more the man . . .

. . . I have given suck, and know
How tender 'tis to love the babe that milks me:
I would, while it was smiling in my face,
Have plucked my nipple from its boneless gums
And dashed the brains out, had I so sworn
As you have done to this.

7   Here's a knocking indeed

Act 2 Scene 3, lines 1–25

PORTER: Here's a knocking indeed; if a man were porter of hell-gate, he should have old turning the key. [*Knock*] Knock, knock, knock. Who's there i'th'name of Beelzebub? Here's a farmer that hanged himself on th'expectation of plenty . . . [*Knock*] Knock, knock. Who's there in th'other devil's name? Faith, here's an equivocator that could swear in both the scales against either scale, who committed treason enough for God's sake, yet could not equivocate to heaven . . . [*Knock*] knock, knock, knock. . . . but this place is too cold for hell. I'll devil-porter it no further . . . [*Opens door*]

Enter MACDUFF *and* LENNOX

MACDUFF: Was it so late, friend, ere you went to bed,
That you do lie so late?

PORTER: Faith, sir, we were carousing till the second cock, and drink, sir, is a great provoker of three things.

MACDUFF: What three things does drink especially provoke?

PORTER: Marry, sir, nose-painting, sleep, and urine. Lechery, sir it provokes, and unprovokes: it provokes the desire, but it takes away the performance . . .

8   Your royal father's murdered

Act 2 Scene 3, lines 89–113

DONALBAIN: What is amiss?

MACBETH: You are, and do not know't.
The spring, the head, the fountain of your blood
Is stopped, the very source of it is stopped.

MACDUFF: Your royal father's murdered.

MALCOLM: Oh, by whom?

LENNOX: Those of his chamber, as it seemed, had done't.
Their hands and faces were all badged with blood,
So were their daggers which, unwiped, we found
Upon their pillows. They stared and were distracted;
No man's life was to be trusted with them.

MACBETH: O, yet I do repent me of my fury
That I did kill them.

MACDUFF: Wherefore did you so?

. . .

MACBETH
        Here lay Duncan,
His silver skin laced with his golden blood
And his gashed stabs looked like a breach in nature,
For ruin's wasteful entrance . . .
        . . . Who could refrain
That had a heart to love and in that heart
Courage to make's love known?

9   Fly, good Fleance, fly, fly, fly!

Act 3 Scene 3, lines 1–21 (not all) and Act 4 Scene 2, lines 70–83 (not all)

FIRST MURDERER: But who did bid thee join with us?

THIRD MURDERER: Macbeth.

SECOND MURDERER: He needs not our mistrust, since he delivers
Our offices and what we have to do
To the direction just.

FIRST MURDERER [*to* THIRD]: Then stand with us.
The west yet glimmers with some streaks of day;
Now spurs the lated traveller apace
To gain the timely inn and near approaches
The subject of our watch

. . .

Enter BANQUO *and* FLEANCE, *with a torch.*

SECOND MURDERER: A light, a light!

THIRD MURDERER: 'Tis he.

FIRST MURDERER: Stand to't

BANQUO: It will rain tonight.

FIRST MURDERER: Let it come down.

Murderers attack. FIRST MURDERER *strikes out the light.*

BANQUO: O, treachery!
Fly, good Fleance, fly, fly, fly!
Thou mayst revenge – O slave!

. . .

LADY MACDUFF: Whither should I fly?
I have done no harm. But I remember now
I am in this earthly world where to do harm
Is often laudable, to do good sometime
Accounted dangerous folly . . .

Enter Murderers
        What are these faces?

A MURDERER: Where is your husband?

LADY MACDUFF: I hope in no place so unsanctified
Where such as thou may fond him.

A MURDERER: He's a traitor.

SON: Thou liest, thou shag-haired villain.

A MURDERER: What, you egg!
Young fry of treachery!

Kills him

SON: He has killed me, mother,
Run away, I pray you.

10   A loving couple?

Act 1 Scene 7, lines 54–59 and Act 5 Scene 1, lines 27–44

LADY MACBETH: . . . I have given suck, and know
How tender 'tis to love the babe that milks me:
I would, while it was smiling in my face,
Have plucked my nipple from its boneless gums
And dashed the brains out, had I so sworn
As you have done to this.

Act 1 Scene 7, lines 54–59

LADY MACBETH: Yet here's a spot . . . Out damned spot! Out, I say! Why then 'tis time
to do't. Hell is murky. Fie, my lord, fie, a soldier, and afeard? What need we fear? Who
knows it, when none can call our power to account? Yet who would have thought the old
man to have had so much blood in him? . . . The Thane of Fife had a wife. Where is she
now? What, will these hands ne'er be clean? No more o'that. My lord, no more o'that.
You mar all with this starting . . . Here's the smell of the blood still; all the perfumes of
Arabia will not sweeten this little hand. O, O, O.

Act 5 Scene 1, lines 27–44 (most of)

11   Unmanned in folly

Act 3 Scene 4, lines 44–73 (most of)

Enter the Ghost of Banquo

. . .

ROSS: . . . Please't your highness
To grace us with your noble company?

MACBETH: The table's full.

LENNOX: Here is a place reserved, sir.

MACBETH: Where?

LENNOX: Here, my good lord. What is't that moves your highness?

MACBETH: Which of you have done this?

LORDS: What, my good lord?

MACBETH: Thou canst not say I did it; never shake
Thy gory locks at me!

. . .

LADY MACBETH: Sit, worthy friends, My lord is often thus,
And hath been since his youth. Pray you, keep seat.
The fit is momentary; upon a thought
He will again be well. If much you note him
You shall offend him and extend his passion.
Feed, and regard not. [*To* MACBETH] Are you a man?

MACBETH: Ay, and a bold one, that dare look on that
Which might appal the devil.

LADY MACBETH: O proper stuff!
This is the very painting of your fear;
This is the air-drawn dagger which you said
Led you to Duncan . . .

. . .

What, quite unmanned in folly?

12   Blood . . . blood . . . blood

Act 3 Scene 4, lines 122–132, 136–138

MACBETH: It will have blood they say: blood will have blood.
Stones have been known to move and trees to speak.
Augures, and understood relations, have
By maggot-pies, and choughs, and rooks brought forth
The secret'st man of blood. What is the night?

LADY MACBETH: Almost at odds with morning, which is which.

MACBETH: How sayst thou that Macduff denies his person
At our great bidding?

LADY MACBETH: Did you send to him, sir?

. . .

MACBETH: There's not one of them but in his house
I keep a servant feed. I will tomorrow –
And betimes I will – to the weird sisters.

. . .

MACBETH: I am in blood
Stepped in so far that should I wade no more,
Returning were as tedious as go o'er . . .

13   Macbeth shall never vanquished be

Act 4 Scene 1, lines 68–94

Thunder. Enter FIRST APPARITION, *an armed head.*

MACBETH: Tell me, thou unknown power –

FIRST APPARITION: Macbeth, Macbeth, Macbeth: Beware Macduff,
Beware the Thane of Fife. Dismiss me. Enough. [*Descends*]

MACBETH: Whate'er thou art, for thy good caution, thanks;
Thou has harped my fear aright. But one word more –

FIRST WITCH: He will not be commanded. Here's another,
More potent than the first.

Thunder. Enter SECOND APPARITION, *a bloody child.*

SECOND APPARITION: Macbeth, Macbeth, Macbeth

. . .

Be bloody, bold and resolute; laugh to scorn
The power of man, for none of woman born
Shall harm Macbeth. [*Descends*]

Enter THIRD APPARITION, *a child crowned with a tree in his hand.*

MACBETH: What is this,
That rises like the issue of a king
And wears upon his baby-brow the round
And top of sovereignty?

ALL THE WITCHES: Listen, but speak not to't.

THIRD APPARITION: Be lion-mettled, proud, and take no care
Who chafes, who frets, or where conspirers are.
Macbeth shall never vanquished be until
Great Birnam Wood to high Dunsinane hill
Shall come against him. [*Descends*]

14   Every sin that has a name

Act 4 Scene 3, lines 57–73

A

MALCOLM: I grant him bloody,
Luxurious, avaricious, false, deceitful,
Sudden, malicious, smacking of every sin
That has a name. But there's no bottom, none,
In my voluptuousness: your wives, your daughters,
Your matrons, and your maids could not fill up
The cistern of my lust, and my desire
All continent impediments would o'erbear
That did oppose my will. Better Macbeth,
Than such as one to reign.

MACDUFF: Boundless intemperance
In nature is a tyranny; it hath been
Th'untimely emptying of the happy throne
And fall of many kings. But fear not yet
To take upon you what is yours; you may
Convey your pleasures in a spacious plenty

And yet seem cold. The time you may so hoodwink.
We have willing dames enough . . .

Lines 91–94

B

MALCOLM: The king-becoming graces –
As justice, verity, temp'rance, stableness,
Bounty, perseverance, mercy, lowliness,
Devotion, patience, courage, fortitude . . .

Lines 91–94

15   I have lived long enough

Act 5 Scene 3, lines 11–28

Enter SERVANT.

MACBETH: The devil damn thee black, thou cream-faced loon.
Where got'st thou that goose-look?

SERVANT: There is ten thousand –

MACBETH: Geese, villain?

SERVANT: Soldiers, sir.

MACBETH: Go prick thy face and over-red thy fear,
Thou lily-livered boy. What soldiers, patch?
Death of thy soul, those linen cheeks of thine
Are counsellors to fear. What soldiers, whey-face?

SERVANT: The English force, so please you.

MACBETH: Take thy face hence!

Exit SERVANT.

               Seyton! – I am sick at heart,
When I behold – Seyton, I say! – this push
Will cheer me ever or disseat me now.
I have lived long enough. My way of life
Is fall'n into the sere, the yellow leaf,
And that which should accompany old age,
As honour, love, obedience, troops of friends,
I must not look to have; but in their stead,
Curses, not loud but deep . . .

16   The queen, my lord, is dead

Act 5 Scene 5, lines 15–29, 32–34

MACBETH: Wherefore was that cry?

SEYTON: The queen, my lord, is dead.

MACBETH: She should have died hereafter;
There would have been a time for such a word.
Tomorrow, and tomorrow, and tomorrow
Creeps in this petty pace from day to day

To the last syllable of recorded time;
And all our yesterdays have lighted fools
The way to dusty death. Out, out brief candle,
Life's but a walking shadow, a poor player
That struts and frets his hour upon the stage
And then is hard no more. It is a tale
Told by an idiot, full of sound and fury
Signifying nothing.

Enter a messenger.

MACBETH: Thou com'st to use thy tongue. Thy story quickly.

MESSENGER: Gracious my lord,

. . .

As I did stand my watch upon the hill
I looked towards Birnam and anon methought
The wood began to move.

Section 2: *A Midsummer Night's Dream*

17   Our nuptial hour

1 Act 1 Scene 1 lines 1–19

THESEUS: Now, fair Hyppolyta, our nuptial hour
Draws on apace; four happy days bring in
Another moon – but O, methinks, how slow
This old moon wanes! She lingers my desires,
Like to a step-dame or a dowager
Long withering out a young man's revenue.

HYPPOLYTA: Four days will quickly steep themselves in night;
Four nights will quickly dream away the time;
And the moon, like to a silver bow
New bent in heaven, shall behold the night
Of our solemnities.

. . .

THESEUS: Hyppolyta, I wooed thee with my sword,
And won thy love doing thee injuries.

18   The raging rocks and shivering shocks

Act 1 Scene 2, lines 1–15

*Enter QUINCE the carpenter, and SNUG the joiner, and BOTTOM the weaver, and
FLUTE the bellows-mender, and SNOUT the tinker and STARVELING the tailor.*

QUINCE: Is all our company here?

BOTTOM: You were best to call them generally, man by man, according to the scrip.

QUINCE: Here is the scroll of every man's name which is thought fit through all Athens
to play in our interlude before the Duke and the Duchess on his wedding day at night.

BOTTOM: First, good Peter Quince, say what the play treats on: then read the names of the actors; and so grow to a point.

QUINCE: Marry, our play is 'The most lamentable comedy and most cruel death of Pyramus and Thisbe'.

BOTTOM: A very good piece of work, I assure you, and a merry. Now, good Peter Quince, call forth your actors by the scroll. Masters, spread yourselves . . .

QUINCE: Answer as I call you, Nick Bottom, the weaver?

BOTTOM: Ready. Name what part I am for, and proceed.

19   With thy brawls thou hast disturbed our sport

Act 2 Scene 1, 88–102

> . . . the winds, piping to us in vain,
> As in revenge have sucked up from the sea
> Contagious fogs; which, falling in the land,
> Hath every pelting river made so proud
> That they have overborne their continents.
> The ox hath therefore stretched his yoke in vain,
> The ploughman lost his sweat, and the green corn
> Hath rotted ere his youth attained a beard.
> The fold stands empty in the drowned field,
> And crows are fatted with the murrion flock;
> The nine-men's-morris is filled up with mud,
> And the quaint mazes in the wanton green
> For lack of tread are undistinguishable.
> The human mortals want their winter cheer;
> No night is now with hymn or carol blessed.

20   I'll follow you

Act 3 Scene 1, lines 83–93

FLUTE   O –
[*as Thisbe*]
As true as truest horse that yet would never tire.

Enter BOTTOM *with the ass head* [*as Pyramus*] *and* PUCK.

BOTTOM [*as Pyramus*]: If I were fair, fair Thisbe, I were only thine.

QUINCE: O monstrous! O strange! We are haunted. Pray, masters! Fly, masters! Help!

Clowns all exit.

PUCK: I'll follow you, I'll lead you about around,
> Through bog, through bush, through brake, through
>   briar.
> Some time a horse I'll be, some time a hound,
>   A hog, a headless bear, sometime a fire,
> And neigh and bark and grunt and roar and burn,
>   Like horse, hound hog, bear, fire, at every turn.

21 Doting in idolatry

Various short passages throughout the play

> She, sweet lady, dotes,
> Devoutly dotes, dotes in idolatry . . .
>
> > Lysander to Theseus about Helena's feelings for Demetrius: 1.1.108.

> Helena, adieu!
> As you on him, Demetrius dote on you.
>
> > Lysander to Helena (about Demetrius): 1.1.225.

> . . . as he errs, doting on Hermia's eyes . . .
>
> > Helena on Demetrius: 1.1.230.

> Love looks not with the eyes but with the mind
>
> > Helena: 1.1.234.

> Sleep thou, and I will wind thee in mine arms.
> Fairies be gone, and be all ways away.
> So doth the woodbine the sweet honeysuckle
> Gently entwist; the female ivy so
> Enrings the barky fingers of the elm.
> O, how I love thee! How I dote on thee!
>
> > Titania to Bottom: 4.1.42.

> O Helen, goddess, nymph, perfect, divine!
> To what, my love, shall I compare thine eyne?
> Crystal is muddy! O, how ripe in show
> Thy lips, those kissing cherries, tempting grow!
> That pure congealed white, high Taurus' snow,
> Fanned with the eastern wind, turns to a crow
> When thou holds't up thy hand. O, let me kiss
> This princess of pure white, this seal of bliss!
>
> > Demetrius to Helena: 3.2.136.

22 My mistress with a monster is in love

Act 3 Scene 2, lines 6–26 (most of)

> PUCK: My mistress with a monster is in love.
>
> . . .
>
> A crew of patches, rude mechanicals,
> That work for bread upon Athenian stalls,
> Were met together to rehearse a play . . .
> The shallowest thick-skin of that barren sort,
> Who Pyramus presented, in their sport
> Forsook his scene and entered in a brake,
> When I did him at this advantage take:
> An ass's nole I fixed on his head.
> Anon his Thisbe must be answered,
> And forth my mimic comes. When they him spy –
> As wild geese that the creeping fowler eye,

Or russet-pated choughs, many in sort,
Rising and cawing at the gun's report,
Sever themselves and madly sweep the sky –
So at his sight away his fellows fly . . .

23   Helena: a character study

Act 3 Scene 2, lines 198–211

HELENA: Is all the counsel that we two have shared,
The sisters' vows, the hours that we have spent
When we have chid the hasty-footed time
For parting us – O, is all forgot?
All schooldays' friendship, childhood innocence?
We, Hermia, like two artificial gods
Have with our needles created both one flower,
Both on one sampler, sitting on one cushion,
Both warbling of one song, both in one key,
As if our hands, our sides, voices, and minds
Had been incorporate. So we grew together
Like to a double cherry, seeming parted,
But yet an union in partition,
Two lovely berries moulded on one stem . . .

24   Lovers' insults

Various lines from Act 3 Scene 2

HELENA [*to* DEMETRIUS]: Out, cur! Thou driv'st me past the
    bounds
Of maiden's patience. Hast thou slain him then?

. . .

O, brave touch!
Could not a worm, an adder do so much?
An adder did it; for with doubler tongue
Than thine, thou serpent, never adder stung.

. . .

HELENA [*to* HERMIA]: You do advance your cunning more and
    more.
When truth kills truth, O devilish-holy fray!

. . .

LYSANDER [*to* HERMIA]: Why seek'st thou me? Could not this
    make thee know
The hate I bare thee made me leave thee so?

. . .

LYSANDER [*to* HERMIA]: Away, you Ethiop! . . .
Hang off, thou cat, thou burr! Vile thing, let loose,
Or I will shake thee from me like a serpent

. . .

Thy love? – out, tawny Tartar, out;
Out loathed medicine! O hated poison, hence!

. . .

HERMIA [*to* HELENA]: O me, you juggler, you canker-blossom,
You thief of love! What, have you come by night
And stol'n my love's heart from him?

. . .

HELENA: Fie, fie, you counterfeit, you puppet, you!

. . .

And though she be but little, she is fierce . . .

25   What vision . . . a most rare vision

Act 4 Scene 1, lines 72–76 and 200–208

TITANIA [*Starting up*]:
My Oberon, what visions have I seen!
Methought I was enamoured of an ass.

OBERON: There lies your love.

TITANIA: How came these things to pass?
O, how mine eyes do loathe his visage now!

. . .

BOTTOM: I have had a most rare vision. I have had a dream, past the wit of man to say
what dream it was. Man is but an ass if he go about to expound this dream. Methought I
was – there is no man can tell what. Methought I was – and methought I had – but man
is but a patched fool if he will offer to say what methought I had. The eye of man hath
not heard, the ear of man hath not seen, man's hand is not able to taste, his tongue to
conceive nor his heart to report what my dream was!

26   A local habitation and a name

Act 5 Scene 1, lines 4–17

THESEUS: Lovers and madmen have such seething brains,
Such shaping fantasies, that apprehend
More than cool reason ever comprehends.
The lunatic, the lover and the poet
Are of imagination all compact:
One sees more devils than vast hell can hold;
That is the madman. The lover, all as frantic,
Sees Helen's beauty in a brow of Egypt.
The poet's eye, in a fine frenzy rolling,
Doth glance from heaven to earth, from earth to heaven;
And as imagination bodies forth
The form of things unknown, the poet's pen
Turns them to shapes, and gives to airy nothing
A local habitation and a name.

27   An anthology of bad verse

Act 5 Scene 1, lines 71–3 and 118–125

THESEUS: What are they like that do play it?

PHILOSTRATE: Hard-handed men that work in Athens here,
Which never laboured in their minds till now

. . .

Enter QUINCE *as prologue.*

QUINCE: If we offend, it is with our good will.
    That you should think, we come not to offend,
But with good will. To show our simple skill,
    That is the true beginning of our end.
Consider then, we come but in despite.
    We do not come as minding to content you,
Our true intent is. All for your delight,
    We are not here. That you should here repent you,
The actors are at hand; and by their show
You shall know all that you are like to know.

THESEUS: This fellow doth not stand upon his points.

LYSANDER: He hath rid his prologue like a rough colt; he knows not the stop. A good moral, my lord; it is not enough to speak, but to speak true.

HYPPOLITA: Indeed, he hath played on this prologue like a child on a recorder – a sound, but not in government.

THESEUS: His speech was like a tangled chain, nothing impaired, but all disordered . . .

28   Thou lob of spirits . . .

Act 5 Scene 1, lines 349–368

PUCK: Now the hungry lion roars,
    And the wolf behowls the moon,
Whilst the heavy ploughman snores,
    All with weary task fordone.
Now the wasted brands do glow,
    While the screech-owl, screeching loud,
Puts the wretch that lies in woe
    In remembrance of a shroud.
Now it is the time of night
    That the graves, all gaping wide,
Every one lets forth his sprite
    In the church-way paths to glide.
And we fairies, that do run
    By the triple Hecate's team
From the presence of the sun,
    Following darkness like a dream,
Now are frolic; not a mouse
Shall disturb this hallowed house.
I am sent with broom before
To sweep the dust behind the door.

Section 3: *Romeo and Juliet*

29   In fair Verona . . .

Prologue and Act 1 Scene 1, lines 5–26

CHORUS: Two households, both alike in dignity,
In fair Verona, where we lay our scene,
From ancient grudge break to new mutiny,
Where civil blood makes civil hands unclean.
From forth the fatal loins of these two foes
A pair of star-crossed lovers take their life,
Whose misadventured piteous overthrows
Do with their death bury their parents' strife.
The fearful passage of their death-marked love:
And the continuance of their parents' rage,
Which, but their children's end, nought could remove,
Is now the two hours' traffic of our stage;
The which if you with patient ears attend,
What here shall miss, our toil shall strive to mend.

. . .

SAMPSON: I strike quickly, being moved.

GREGORY: But thou art not quickly moved to strike.

SAMPSON: A dog of the house of Montague might move me.

GREGORY: To move is to stir; and to be valiant is to stand: therefore if thou art moved, thou runn'st away.

SAMPSON: A dog of that house shall move me to stand. I will take the wall of any man or maid of Montague's.

GREGORY: That shows thee a weak slave, for the weakest goes to the wall.

SAMPSON: True, and therefore women being the weaker sex are ever thrust to the wall: therefore I will push Montague's men from the wall, and thrust his maids to the wall.

GREGORY: The quarrel is between our masters and us their men.

SAMPSON: 'Tis all one. I will show myself a tyrant: when I have fought with the men, I will be civil with the maids, and cut off their maidenheads.

GREGORY: The heads of the maids?

SAMPSON: Ay, the heads of the maids, or their maidenheads, take it in what sense thou wilt.

GREGORY: They must take it in sense that feel it.

SAMPSON: Me they shall feel when I am able to stand, and 'tis known I am a pretty piece of flesh.

30   O brawling love . . . fiend angelical!

Act 1 Scene 1, lines 166–173 and Act 3 Scene 2, lines 73–79

ROMEO: Why then, O brawling love, O loving hate,
O any thing of nothing first create!

O heavy lightness, serious vanity,
Misshapen chaos of well-seeming forms,
Feather of lead, bright smoke, cold fire, sick health,
Still-walking sleep, that is not what it is!
This love feel I, that feel no love in this.

. . .

JULIET: O serpent heart, hid with a flow'ring face!
Did ever dragon keep so fair a cave?
Beautiful tyrant, fiend angelical!
Dove-feathered raven, wolvish-ravening lamb!
Despised substance of divinest show!
Just opposite to what though justly seem'st,
A damned saint, an honourable villain!

31   A fair assembly

Act 1 Scene 2, lines 34–43 and 63–72

CAPULET [*to* SERVANT]: Go, sirrah, trudge about
Through fair Verona, find these persons out
Whose names are written there [*Gives a paper*] and to them say,
My house and welcome on their pleasure stay.

CAPULET *exits.*

SERVANT: Find them out whose names are written here! It is written that the shoemaker should meddle with his yard and the tailor with his last, the fisher with his pencil and the painter with his nets; but I am sent to find those persons here writ, and I can never find what names the writing person hath here write. I must to the learned. In good time!

Enter BENVOLIO *and* ROMEO.

. . .

ROMEO: God-den, good fellow.

SERVANT: God gi' god-den. I pray, sir, can you read?

. . .

ROMEO *reads the letter.*
'Signior Martino and his wife and daughters,
County Anselme and his beauteous sisters,
The lady widow of Vitruvio,
Signior Placentino and his lovely nieces,
Mercutio and his brother Valentine,
Mine uncle Capulet, his wife and daughters,
My fair niece Rosaline, and Livia,
Signior Valentio and his cousin Tybalt,
Lucio and the lively Helena.'
A fair assembly: whither should they come?

SERVANT: Up . . . to our house . . . My master is the great rich Capulet . . .

32 A pretty age

Act 1 Scene 3, lines 11–25 and Act 2 Scene 5, selected lines

LADY CAPULET: . . .
Thou knowest my daughter's of a pretty age.

NURSE: Faith, I can tell her age unto an hour.

LADY CAPULET: She's not fourteen.

NURSE: I'll lay fourteen of my teeth –
And yet to my teen be it spoken, I have but four –
She's not fourteen. How long is it now
To Lammas-tide?

LADY CAPULET: A fortnight and odd days.
NURSE: Even or odd, of all days in the year,
Come Lammas-tide at eve shall she be fourteen.
Susan and she – God rest all Christian souls! –
Were of an age. Well, Susan is with God,
She was too good for me. But as I said,
On Lammas-tide at night shall she be fourteen,
That shall she, marry, I remember it well.
'Tis since the earthquake now eleven years

. . .

JULIET: . . . Though news be sad, yet tell them merrily;

. . .

NURSE: I am a-weary, give me leave a while.
Fie, how my bones ache! What a jaunce have I!

JULIET: I would thou hadst my bones, and I thy news.
Nay, come, I pray thee speak, good, good Nurse, speak.

NURSE: Jesu, what haste! Can you not stay a while?
Do you not see that I am out of breath?

JULIET: How art thou out of breath, when thou hast breath
To say to me that thou are out of breath? . . .

33 Mercutio: a grave man

Act 2 Scene 1, lines 17–29 (Mercutio's lines only) and Act 3 Scene 1, lines 82–83, 89–90, 97–99

A

MERCUTIO: I conjure thee by Rosaline's bright eyes,
But her high forehead and her scarlet lip,
By her fine foot, straight leg, and quivering thigh,
And the demesnes that there adjacent lie,
That in thy likeness thou appear to us.

. . .

This cannot anger him; 'twould anger him
To raise a spirit in his mistress' circle,

Of some strange nature, letting it there stand
Till she had laid it and conjured it down:
That were some spite. My invocation
Is fair and honest: in his mistress name
I conjure only but to raise him up.

Act 2 Scene 1, lines 17–29 (Mercutio's lines only)

B

ROMEO: Hold, Tybalt! Good Mercutio!

TYBALT *stabs* MERCUTIO *and runs away.*

MERCUTIO: I am hurt.
A plague a' both your houses! I am sped.
Is he gone and hath nothing?

BENVOLIO: What, art thou hurt?

MERCUTIO: Ay, ay, a scratch, a scratch, marry, 'tis enough.
Where is my page? Go, villain, fetch a surgeon.

Exit Page.

ROMEO: Courage, man, the hurt cannot be much.

MERCUTIO: No, 'tis not so deep as a well, nor so wide as a church door, but 'tis enough, 'twill serve. Ask for me tomorrow, and you shall find me a grave man . . .

. . .

A plague a' both your houses!
They have made worms' meat of me. I have it,
And soundly too. Your houses!

Act 3 Scene 1, lines 82–83, 89–90, 97–99

34   And palm to palm is holy palmer's kiss

Act 1 Scene 5, lines 93–105 and Act 2 Scene 2, lines 25–55

A

ROMEO: If I profane with my unworthiest hand
This holy shrine, the gentle sin is this,
My lips, two blushing pilgrims, ready stand
To smooth that rough touch with a tender kiss.

JULIET: Good pilgrim, you do wrong your hand too much,
Which mannerly devotion shows in this,
For saints have hands that pilgrims' hands do touch
And palm to palm is holy palmer's kiss.

ROMEO: Have saints not lips, and holy palmers too?

JULIET: Ay, pilgrim, lips that they must use in prayer.

ROMEO: O then, dear saint, let lips do what hands do:
They pray, grant thou, lest faith turn to despair.

JULIET: Saints do not move, though grant for prayers' sake.

ROMEO: Then move not while my prayer's effect I take.

B

ROMEO [*Aside*]:   She speaks.
O speak again, bright angel, for thou art
As glorious to this night, being o'er my head,
As is a winged messenger of heaven
Unto the white-upturned wond'ring eyes
Of mortals that fall back to gaze on him,
When he bestrides the lazy puffing clouds,
And sails upon the bosom of the air.

JULIET: O Romeo, Romeo, wherefore art thou Romeo?
Deny thy father and refuse thy name;
Or if thou wilt not, be but sworn my love,
And I'll no longer be a Capulet.

ROMEO [*Aside*]: Shall I hear more, or shall I speak at this?

JULIET: 'Tis but thy name that is my enemy;
Thou art thyself, though not a Montague.
What's Montague? It is nor hand nor foot,
Nor arm nor face, nor any other part
Belonging to a man. O be some other name!
What's in a name? That which we call a rose
By any other word would smell as sweet;
So Romeo would, were he not Romeo called . . .

. . .

ROMEO: I take thee at thy word:
Call me but love, and I'll be new baptised . . .

35   Good morrow, father

Act 2 Scene 3, lines 1–12

FRIAR LAWRENCE: The grey-haired morn smiles on the frowning night,
Check'ring the eastern clouds with streaks of light;
And fleckled darkness, like a drunkard, reels
From forth day's path and Titan's fiery wheels:
Now ere the sun advance his burning eye,
The day to cheer, and night's dank dew to dry,
I must upfill this osier cage of ours
With baleful weeds, and precious-juiced flowers.
The earth that's nature's mother is her tomb;
What is her burying grave, that is her womb;
And from her womb children of divers kind
We sucking on her natural bosom find.

36 Mistress minion you

Act 3 Scene 5, lines 149–168

CAPULET: How how, how how, chopt-logic. What is this?
'Proud', and 'I thank you', and 'I thank you not',
And yet, 'not proud', mistress minion you?
Thank me no thanking, nor proud me no prouds,
But fettle your fine joints 'gainst Thursday next,
To go with Paris to Saint Peter's Church,
Or I will drag thee on a hurdle thither.
Out, you green-sickness carrion! Out, you baggage!
You tallow-face!

. . .

Hang thee, young baggage, disobedient wretch!
I tell thee what: get thee to church a' Thursday,
Or never after look me in the face.
Speak not, reply not, do not answer me!
My fingers itch. Wife, we scarce thought us blest
That God had lent us but this only child,
But now I see this one is one too much,
And that we have a curse on having her.
Out on her, hilding!

37 Take thou this vial

Act 4 Scene 1, lines 78–85 and 93–106

JULIET: O bid me leap, rather than marry Paris,
From off the battlements of any tower,
Or walk in thievish ways, or bid me lurk
Where serpents are; chain me with roaring bears,
Or hide me nightly in a charnel-house,
O'ercovered quite with dead man's rattling bones,
With reeky shanks and yellow chapless skulls;
Or bid me go into a new-made grave,
And hide me with a dead man in his shroud . . .

FRIAR: Take thou this vial, being then in bed,
And this distilling liquor drink thou off,
When presently through all thy veins shall run
A cold and drowsy humour; for no pulse
Shall keep his native progress, but surcease;
No warmth, no breath shall testify thou livest;
The roses in thy lips and cheeks shall fade
To wanny ashes, thy eyes' windows fall,
Like Death when he shuts up the day of life;
Each part, deprived of supple government,
Shall stiff and stark and cold appear like death
And in this borrowed likeness of shrunk death
Thou shalt continue two and forty hours,
And then awake as from a pleasant sleep.

38 Farewell! God knows when we shall meet again

Act 4 Scene 3, lines from Juliet's speech 14–58

> Farewell! God know when we shall meet again.
> I have a faint cold fear thrills through my veins
> That almost freezes up the heat of life
>
> . . .
>
> What if this mixture do not work at all?
> Shall I be married then tomorrow morning?
> No, no, this shall forbid it; lie thou there.
> [*Lays down the dagger*]
> What if it be a poison which the Friar
> Subtly hath ministered to have me dead,
> Lest in this marriage he should be dishonoured,
> Because he married me before to Romeo?
>
> . . .
>
> How if, when I am laid into the tomb,
> I wake before the time that Romeo
> Come to redeem me? There's a fearful point!
> Shall I not then be stifled in the vault,
> To whose foul air no healthsome air breathes in,
> And there die strangled till my Romeo comes?
> Or if I live, is it not very like
> The horrible conceit of death and night,
> Together with the terror of the place
>
> . . .
>
> Where bloody Tybalt, yet but green in earth,
> Lies fest'ring in his shroud, where, as they say,
> At some hours in the night spirits resort –
> Alack, alack . . .
> O, if I wake, shall I not be distraught,
> Environed with all these hideous fears,
> And madly play with my forefathers' joints,
> And pluck the mangled Tybalt from his shroud . . .

39 She's dead, deceased, dead

Act 4 Scene 5, lines 19–33

> LADY CAPULET: O me, O me, my child, my only life!
> Revive, look up, or I will die with thee.
> Help, help! Call help.
>
> *Enter* CAPULET.
>
> CAPULET: For shame, bring Juliet forth, her lord is come.
>
> NURSE: She's dead, deceased, she's dead, alack the day!
>
> LADY CAPULET: Alack the day, she's dead, she's dead, she's dead!
>
> CAPULET: Hah, let me see her. Out alas, she's cold,

Her blood is settled, and her joints are stiff:
Life and those lips have long been separated;
Death lies upon her like an untimely frost
Upon the sweetest flower of the field.

NURSE: O lamentable day!

LADY CAPULET: O woeful time!

CAPULET: Death that hath tane her hence to make me wail
Ties up my tongue and will not let me speak.

Enter FRIAR LAWRENCE *and* PARIS.

FRIAR LAWRENCE: Come, is the bride ready to go to church?

40 Who calls so loud?

Act 5 Scene 1, lines 57–75

APOTHECARY: Who calls so loud?

ROMEO: Come, hither, man. I see that thou art poor.
Hold, there is forty ducats; let me have
A dram of poison, such soon-speeding gear
As will disperse itself through all the veins,
That the life-weary taker may fall dead,
And that the trunk may be discharged of breath
As violently as hasty powder fired
Doth hurry from the fatal cannon's womb.

APOTHECARY: Such mortal drugs I have, but Mantua's law
Is death to any he that utters them.

ROMEO: Art thou so bare and full of wretchedness,
And fearest to die? Famine is in thy cheeks,
Need and oppression starveth in thy eyes,
Contempt and beggary hangs upon thy back;
The world is not thy friend, nor the world's law,
The world affords no law to make thee rich;
Then be not poor, but break it and take this.

APOTHECARY: My poverty, but not my will, consents.

41 O Brother Montague

Act 5 Scene 3, lines 296–310

PRINCE: . . . Capulet, Montague?
See what a scourge is laid upon your hate,
That heaven finds means to kills your joys with love!
And I for winking at your discords too
Have lost a brace of kinsmen. All are punished.

CAPULET: O brother Montague, give me thy hand.
This is my daughter's jointure, for no more
Can I demand.

MONTAGUE: But I can give thee more,

For I will raise her statue in pure gold,
That whiles Verona by that name is known,
There shall no figure by such rate be set
As that of true and faithful Juliet.

CAPULET: As rich as Romeo's by his lady's lie,
Poor sacrifices of our enmity!

PRINCE: A·glooming peace this morrow with it brings,
The sun for sorrow will not show his head.
Go hence to have more talk of these sad things;
Some shall be pardoned, and some punished:
For never was a story of more woe
Than this of Juliet and her Romeo.